MW00718446

A piece of Nese:
Made in Oakland

Author trinese robinson
facebook

ms.trineserobinson@gmail.com

Hope you enjoy
Story Love
Nese
xoxo

A piece of Nese: Made in Oakland

Trinese Robinson

© 2017 Trinese Robinson
All rights reserved.

ISBN: 0692794549
ISBN 13: 9780692794548
Library of Congress Control Number: 2016921290
A piece of Nese..Made in Oakland, Sacramento, CALIFORNIA

Dedication

This book is dedicated to my family. I love you!

Contents

CHAPTER 1

East Oakland

Oakland...the East, the West, and the North...highways 580 and 880...Warriors, Raiders, and the A's...the Town

I'M TWELVE YEARS old, light skinned with long hair down to my butt. I am mixed; my mother is black and Creole, and my father is black, Italian, and Cherokee Indian. I grew up being called names such as "mixed chick" and "half-breed"; you name it, and I guarantee I was called it.

I always felt that I wasn't the finest but I wasn't the ugliest. To my little sister and me, being told we were pretty was nice. But we also had our fair share of haters. "You think you're cute." "You think you look good." Or "You're stuck up." Being told this by strangers wasn't anything new to me.

If I got paid for every time I was called light skinned or Red Bone or someone asked me, "What are you mixed with?" man, I would be a millionaire.

When I was a little girl, I would ride on the 580 freeway, and I would look up at the Morman temple and dream it was my castle and I was a princess, something out of a Disney movie.

I quickly realized that life is not a fairy tale, and it's just a dream. So wake up, Nese, and get out of la-la land, because the real world is not a joke. It is not a game.

Hello, and welcome to my world! The world of Trinese, a.k.a. Nese.

I grew up living in the Bay Area—East Oakland, to be exact—in an OK middle-class neighborhood. My block wasn't too bad. But hearing gunshots wasn't anything new, or seeing people selling drugs right off the main strip in Oakland (the Town) Foothill Boulevard. Side shows and fast cars driving by were the norm. Candy paint and old-school cars.

A lot of the girls wanted a cool, cute dude who had a car that had candy paint and rims, who had money and dressed cute and who was also well known. I never really tripped off that; I wanted my own. I always thought, it's not my car and money, my name is not on the title, so why trip off other people's stuff? I'm happy for them, but I wanted my own. When I was in junior high school, I got a job.

On Friday night, I would watch *Miami Vice* with my sister, and at least twice, someone would run down the side of our house and drop his or her gun, or "gat," as we called it in the eighties. *Miami Vice* cops would be shooting on TV, and there would be a real-life shooting going on outside when the guy dropped his gun at my window while running from the police.

Man, I was young and didn't really understand how dangerous life could be.

I met this young guy walking to the store; he was about three years older than me. We exchanged numbers, something I never did, but he seemed like a nice and OK young man. He told me he had just moved to Oakland from out of state.

We talked on the phone; he would pick me up, and I showed him the Bay Area. We became cool friends. After about six months of talking on the phone, going out to eat, going shopping, going to the lake, going to the movies, getting ice cream, and just having fun, fun, fun, we were best friends.

One day he told me I should be his girlfriend. I said OK. He was really sweet and respectable.

One day I called him, but no answer. For days, no answer.

As a kid I always loved to read, and my parents gave us the newspaper when we were young. I loved the cartoon comics. So as I was reading the newspaper, in the local section in the Oakland Tribune, I saw a picture of him in an article about how he got robbed, gunned down, and killed in his car. I was like, what the f***? Excuse my French.

He was not from here; he had a lot of money. His family was rich, they owned businesses, and he drove a Mercedes Benz and had nice jewelry and clothes. And when you have it going on, you look like fresh meat to some people, and you are their prey.

I was really sad and depressed about his death but at the same time glad that I wasn't in the car with him, because he would give me rides here and there. My boyfriend was dead and at a very young age. RIP—so sad!

In my teenage years in East Oakland, we would go to Eastmont Mall and go to the movies there or to the Century Theatre or to Bayfair Mall. We would go to the Grand Prix Arcade and play video games and race cars after the movies, head over to Denny's to eat, and then go home.

There was gun violence, but kids weren't killing kids every day, all day, in broad daylight like now. Kids had somewhat of a value for life. Back in the day, kids would fight. If you were a punk, you would set up someone to get jumped, but you were later friends after the fight, for the most part. Or you would never be friends again, and the girls would just look at you crazy, talk about you behind your back, and roll their eyes. Things have surely changed.

In the late eighties, a lot of people were selling drugs, and a lot of people became dope fiends. When I look back, I realize that's when Oakland started to change. Growing up, I knew people on drugs, and a lot of kids sold them to make money. I know a lot of people from elementary school, junior high school, and high school who are dead now. It got to a point where I had three or four photo albums of just obituaries that I collected to look back on over the years. It was a shame. The paper started to create maps of all the murder victims each year.

I grew up in Oakland with my mom and dad, a middle-class married couple, and a sister and brother. Both my parents had jobs; they owned their home and were very loving and caring parents, and I was blessed to have parents and a family that really took good care of us kids.

We had a nice house, and we were raised in a very strict household. We were raised to go to school, do homework, get good grades, clean up, do chores, work hard, not be lazy, cook and clean, wash our own clothes, get a job, respect our elders, read the Bible, and go to the hall. A lot of things I liked about the religion, but I didn't like that people judged me, and that made me not go as much when I got older.

I really didn't have a problem with any of that, because it made me the woman I am today, but because my parents were so strict, I didn't experience a lot of things other kids did. I never spent the night at anyone's house, if they were not family.

My day-one people I grew up with were my cousins Michelle and Mark and Auntie Jackie at Grandma Gilda's house, with Uncle Charlie, Auntie Didi, and Lil Charlie. I hung with my cousins Vicky and Pat, Mike, Tonya, and Trinian, at the top of Kelley Hill in Hayward, California. Tosha, Yoshii, and Erica got me out of the house, or I hung at the houses of my best friends—Jackie, Nicole, and Shelley—because their parents were not as strict as mine.

Going over to my auntie Tammy's house was an escape. She would spoil me and my sister rotten! The main place I loved to go was to my grandmother Mamaul's house in the Oakland Hills. We had our own room, so that was cool!

All I would say was, "I can't wait till I grow up." Wish I had known then what I know now, trust me!

At the end of the day, I have to thank my parents for the job they did, and now I see what I put them through, with my kids. It's the big payback, but ten times over. Yep! That's what I get.

Water-balloon fights and ice-cream trucks, playing double Dutch outside, and talking on the house phone on three-way—hey, those were the days. I had just graduated elementary and was going to junior high. Who knew death would knock?

CHAPTER 2

—⚭—

Grandmother Ella, a.k.a. Mamaul

A grandmother's love stays in your heart forever

He is healing the broken hearted one,
binding up their painful spots.

—Psalms 147:3

I HAD THE very best grandmothers, both of them. One of them was killed, murdered, and I will never forget her as long as I live. She is a part of me, and she instilled values in my life that I stand by and always will. Her name was Ella, a Creole gal from New Orleans.

It's been over thirty years, but it still feels like yesterday. When I was in elementary school, my grandmother was my role model. She was very beautiful, smart, and educated. She was very active in the community and church. She invested in businesses and real estate and was rich. She had a home in Oakland Hills. She could cook, and till this very day, she was by far the best cook besides my mom and aunt I have known.

Mamaul had a room for her shoes, furs, and lots of jewelry, and she drove a Caddy. I wanted to be just like her. She stressed college, and all she would talk about was how she was going to pay her grandkids' way, no matter what.

My sister and I had our own room at her house, with a California king mattress. She treated us like princesses, served us in bed on platters with her fancy dishes, and made homemade cookies and ice cream. At Mamaul's house we would play dress-up, curl our hair, and put on make-up, perfume, jewelry, furs, and high heels, my sis and I. We always had a ball!

We would spend the weekend, and on Saturday she would say, "Hey, we got to go get the rent checks" (she was a landlord). So we would ride around, get checks, and then go to the bank. She would deposit money into our account for college, and then we would go shopping. I loved it. She was the best.

My grandmother called me every day, but when she didn't call me on my birthday, I just felt she was dead. I told my mom, "My grandmother is dead. She would have called me!"

My mom asked, "Why would you say she's dead? Why would you say that?"

I called her home phone over and over again, but no answer. I asked my mom, "Please take me over to her house." We got in the car and drove to my grandmother's house.

Driving up the hill to her house, we saw the house surrounded by police, ambulances, and yellow tape. My mom jumped out of the car, screaming, and I did too. The police told me to sit down; they were taking her body out.

She was killed in the bedroom she gave my sister and me, murdered in her own home. Her body passed me in a bag, zipped up. I sneaked into the room, and my tennis shoe filled with some of her blood. I was in total shock. This was not the movies, and yes, I saw a part of my grandmother's brain on the floor. My eyes felt as if they were going to explode out of my face. I couldn't believe it.

I was devastated! My whole family was, and I miss her so much. I always think about what our lives would be like if she were never murdered. She died a very violent death from many hammer blows to the head and then being shot.

My Mamaul didn't allow us to call her "grandma"; we had to call her Mamaul. She taught me to be pretty on the inside and outside and treat others as I want to be treated. She wanted us to be owners of properties and a franchise. "Kill them with kindness" is what she always said, and "Always act like a lady!"

While the family was in the house, wondering who killed my grandmother, my stepuncle took me to the Baskin-Robbins my grandmother owned on 104th Street in Oakland for ice cream. "For your birthday," he said.

The first question he asked me was, "Who do you think killed your grandmother?"

I said, "I don't know."

Little did I or anybody else in the house know my stepuncle was the one who killed my grandmother. And he asked me who did it—the nerve he had! He was later caught; he got twenty years but did ten. I never thought that was fair, but they say that's justice. I was like, wow, she's dead, and he's out starting a new life? Only God can judge.

My grandmother had a double funeral, one in Oakland and the second in New Orleans, where she was born.

My mom took my grandmother's death very hard. I can't imagine her pain. I know I felt a deep knife in my heart. When my grandmother was killed, I lost her, but I also lost a piece of my mom too. It was a double whammy! My mom suffered from depression, and at a young age, I had a small piece of depression too.

For my sixth-grade graduation, my grandmother gave me money, $250, to get all my clothes and stuff for graduation in June. She came to my graduation and told me she was very proud, and the next month she was gone. That was my last great memory of her.

Till this day I miss her and cherish my memories of her. When I see people abuse or not care about their grandparents, I wish I could bring back all my grandparents.

July 18, the day before my birthday.

RIP, Mamaul. Miss you and love you!

CHAPTER 3

---❦---

Bret Harte Junior High

Where it all started…the school named us Mr. and Mrs. Bobcat…
the school couple

I WAS STARTING junior high; I was nervous and excited to meet new friends
and start school. My parents and aunt bought me a lot of nice school
clothes, and I was really happy about that!

When I first started school, I was in the gifted classes, and I soon realized that those classes were not that easy and I had to put effort into my
work. I also noticed there weren't a lot of cool kids in those classes. So I

started to not work as hard and asked for my classes to be switched. As soon as the classes were switched, I was passing with As and Bs, and I had a lot of fun with my friends.

Overall, I had a lot of friends, but there were also at least ten girls who hated me for no reason, and they made it known every day. So that made it hard for me to want to go to school. I was bullied by older girls and threatened, especially if one of them had a boyfriend and he was cool with me. That only made things worse.

One girl knew where I lived, so she showed up at my house and knocked on the door and said they wanted to jump me. So I said, "Hold on a sec." My dad was a carpenter, so I went to the closet where he kept his tools and plugged up his power saw and opened the door and turned it on! That girl ran to the car! I know, I know, that's really crazy, but I was tired of it and scared, and nobody was home at the time but me.

The next day, the girl wanted to fight me, so she followed me to my gym class. Next thing you know, it's a brawl, at least twenty people fighting, and someone locked the main door so no adults could come in.

The girl's mom worked for the DA and wanted to press charges against me. I explained she had come to my house the day before, and on top of that, I never had a problem with her, and as a matter of fact, I didn't really even know this girl at all.

The crazy part is I woke up that morning and told my mom, "Mom, I'm getting suspended today. I have tried and tried, but these girls keep messing with me for months. I got to defend myself."

She said, "Well, you know that if that happens, you will be in trouble and on punishment."

I said, "I will have to take the consequences."

I got suspended for a week, but after that fight, nobody messed with me. Some of the girls and I became cool, not friends but cool—we didn't have any problems anymore—and I was happy about that. Got tired of watching my back.

Out of all the schools in my life, Bret Harte was my favorite. There was a 7-Eleven store on the property, and the students ran it. A lot of my friends today are from that school. Most of the time we keep in contact on Facebook. Some of my friends I would hang with were BEV, Ashonti, Latonya, Valencia, Kimberly, Lashonda, Denise, Tamika, Tracy, my family Tantosha, my sis Brandi, Charlene, Jacquce, Rasheda, Ava, and Karen, to name just a few. We would have fun; times were different then. Kids really were kids and had fun, and gun violence was not how it is today.

My BFFs were Ashonti, Valencia, and Kimberly. Shonni and V sometimes didn't get along for some reason, which put me in a bad spot in the middle of it. All three girls had a very special relationship with me, and till this day we have maintained a thirty-plus-year friendship, which is very odd in this day and age.

Ashonti's mother, whom I called Moms, passed away, but before she did, she was very close with me and encouraged and prayed with me a lot about all the bad things I had going on in life and to never give up hope, faith, and love for God! I miss and love her dearly.

My friend Kimberly is very special to me. I can tell her anything, with no judgments! She knows me like a book. Love you, Kimmy!

Now my best friend V, Ms. Valencia, I told her I liked Monie and not to tell, but she did, and that's how I ended up married with four kids by my eighth-grade boyfriend. I always told her that! V is my sister from another motha, and I love her mother as well!

I'm very blessed to have great friends, so many of them! Because of Bret Harte, I have my family. Who knew that was going to happen? We were only twelve years old. Wow.

After school, Monie, his cousin Dae, and I would hang out. Sometimes his other cousin Day or his cousin Jaqaun would be there. My BF Jackie was talking to Day, and my cousin E would hang with us too. Those were the days: no worries and no bills.

When I was thirteen years old, Monie said to me, "I want you to have my son," while I was waiting for the bus.

I said, "Boy, I'm thirteen years old, going on fourteen. I'm going to McDonald's on Fruitvale. We are way too young for that, way too young." I started to laugh so hard. "Boy, I'm not having no kids! You are crazy, ha-ha-ha-ha-ha."

He said, "Yes, we are."

I told him, "Oh no, we are not. That would mean I would have to see you for the rest of my life, and I'm not doing that."

So he said, "F*** you, b****," and he walked off mad and upset.

I could see he was serious, too, but I knew my dad would have literally killed me, and I'm not stupid. I always said to my dad it takes two to tango, and he would say, "You don't want to get pregnant."

After junior high school, we broke up, but after about a year, we got back together. I had just gotten out of a relationship with someone else, and so had he. We both were in high school, and Monie was a football player, quarterback #17 at Skyline.

Then I got pregnant in my senior year!

When I did get pregnant, I was scared to tell my dad. I said, "Dad, I'm pregnant and seventeen."

He said, "Oh, I guess you two to tango!"

I felt I had let my family down by being a teenage mom. I decided I would go to school, work, and take care of my son and my life would be all about my son. My teenage life was over.

When I was young, I wanted to do so many things, but I didn't know exactly what. I wanted to be a nurse. My sister had cancer at a very young age, so when I saw nurses help kids in the hospital, I said to myself, "I want to do that." I also wanted to be a writer. I wrote poems and stories in junior high and high school and won a scholarship to college, but I didn't have support to go out of state, and I was scared to leave with no financial help from my parents.

But before I could follow any of these dreams, I became a mother in twelfth grade. However, because I had a job and did summer school every year and IWE after school before I got pregnant, I was set to graduate on time. I was so glad that years before, I planned to graduate a year early, so that helped me graduate on time, and I did!

Bret Harte was the start of a relationship, Mr. and Mrs. Bobcat, that ended up being the story of Mr. and Mrs. Robinson.

Who knew? Here's a picture of Monie, Little Monie, and me.

CHAPTER 4

— ✂ —

Run Away, Nese

*No looking back, far away from here, far away
from here, far away from here, just jump in a
taxi cab, pack a bag, and get away fast.*

—KINDRED THE FAMILY SOUL

MY PARENTS WERE super strict, and I couldn't really do jack. They were
Jehovah's Witnesses, and even though I never got baptized, I must admit
a lot of what I learned I still apply to this day: Treat others how you want
to be treated. Have respect for your elders. Always be on your best be-
havior. I learned a lot and met sisters and brothers who still have love for
me and are very loving and caring people.

I was in high school then, and I was working, cooking, cleaning, and
helping with my little brother and sister. My grandmother was murdered;
then shortly after, my grandfather died of cancer, my mom had a baby,
and my sister got cancer and had her leg amputated, all within the same
year. I couldn't take the pressure, so I packed a bag and ran away. I
hugged my sister, and I left. I was seventeen.

I stayed at a hotel and motels with my boyfriend. I hated home but
loved home, but home felt like prison. I missed home, and I cried a lot. I
missed my sister. Sometimes I wanted to go back.

Monie would sell drugs at night and go to school during the day. I
hated that; I was scared for him and me. We got an apartment, but that
didn't last long; they found out we were minors.

I had left home almost a year before when I got pregnant with our son. We moved in with his aunt Phaedra. I told him, "It's been a long time, and I should go back home...and you should too. We both should focus on school and get help from our parents."

So I went back home. He was mad, but it was better for the both of us. Monie played football for Skyline High. He was quarterback #7, and he was on his way to college, and I didn't want to mess that up.

One weekend, we went to take our son some pictures, at the mall and he made a stop. He jumped out of the cab and said, "I will call you later."

Later on he did—from jail.

He was set up. I won't go into detail, but he got three years in prison. No senior year, no college, and no NFL. When he got out of prison, he had so many regrets about not making it.

Life doesn't always go as planned.

CHAPTER 5

Jamonie, a.k.a. Monie Hogg the Great

Something he lived by, all family and no friends

MONIE HOGG THE Great: that's what he called himself. He was called Monie Hogg in college by his football teammates, so he kept the name.

He could have gone pro. His friends made it, at least five of them, but he got caught up in the streets and ended up going to prison. My son had a great dad who loved him to pieces, but he had to leave. When he got out, he said that he was never going back to prison, and he never did.

He got out after eighteen months, got off probation, and went to college. He was the first black quarterback at Chabot College in Hayward, California.

We got a place and had a little girl, Ash. Things were looking great! Monie was a good father; he always watched them and played with them. Birth control did not work, and I got pregnant with my third child, Paris, whom I named after my cousin who was murdered. Paris James, RIP, cuz!

We moved in with Grandma to save money so we could buy a house, and a year and a half later, we had baby number four, redhead Nini.

Monie was light skinned; he had a nice complexion, with faded hair. He was very nice looking. He looked like my brother, so men would try to talk to me in front of him, and he had quite a few ladies liking him too, which caused problems.

Monie loved cars, old-school ones: his Cougar, his old-school Caddy. He loved to restore cars. He had a Camaro, a Cougar, a Caddy (Cadillac), and an Oldsmobile, and we had a minivan too.

Monie loved football all his life, at Pop Warner, high school, and college. He wore #7 and #17. He loved his kids, clothes, money, cars, his family, music, and women. Sometimes he was a single husband, but I always had his back, and I always forgave him.

My husband was very funny, smart, and talented, and I always said he could do something positive with his life. He called me a square bear; he told me to stay square. He kept secrets and always told me, "It is best if you don't know anything." True, you know; sometimes it is best, but if you don't know, then no one will tell you about it, and you're in the dark. Sometimes that's not cool either.

My job was to take care of the kids, work, cook, clean, and do family stuff. He would leave, and I wouldn't have a clue as to what he was doing or whom he was with. It put a worry on me. I would always pray! Pray, pray, pray that he wouldn't get killed out there in the streets.

During the day he would take the kids to school and pick them up. He would watch them. He loved the kids so much; they were closer to him than they were to me. They all loved him so, so much. He never showed the kids his lifestyle, and he stressed school, sports, and music.

He loved music! He loved all music, but he loved rap music so much so he would do raps at different studios in the Bay. Eventually we ended up getting a studio in the basement, which turned out to be a horrible idea.

About a year before he was killed, he was turning his life around. He told me he was tired and wanted to change his life, and I could tell he did in a major way. He started by building a closer relationship with God. He totally changed, and I loved the man he was becoming.

CHAPTER 6

— ✄ —

October 16, 2005

"So Many Tears," by 2Pac

IT WAS SUNDAY, October 16. I was babysitting my niece and nephew and watching my kids. We were having fun downloading music on CDs, and my aunt was helping us. We were watching movies with the kids, little kids running around in and out of the house, eating snacks and cookies and kicking it.

My husband asked me to go and get some Giant Burgers for him and his patna (friend) in the studio downstairs, so I said OK. I came back and brought him his food, and he was watching TV in the studio.

A few hours later, he was hungry again, and we ran out of CDs, so I went to Best Buy, got some CDs, and headed to KFC to get some chicken. When I got back to the house, everybody started making plates, and we started making CDs with music again.

My nephew was about two years old at the time. He never would let me hold him; he always wanted his uncle. That made me kind of jealous. He-he. I love my niece KK and nephew. While Monie and I were talking, my little nephew stole a piece of chicken off Monie's plate and ran. We didn't notice until he looked down and it was gone. We found Little Doodah in the corner, and he had already eaten the chicken. We cracked up.

My sister came and picked up her kids, and I started to wash clothes. Monie kept telling me to go to the casino, somewhere I loved to go, but something was telling me to stay. He had bought me a Victoria's

Secret sweat suit two days before, so he said, "Let's go to the mall in San Francisco and get some shoes that would match your sweat suit."

"But," I said, "it's five o'clock, and the mall closes at six. It's Sunday! Let's go tomorrow when I get off work. Plus I really needed to wash my kids' school uniforms."

"Let me help you fold."

"No, that's OK."

"Let me help you with something, please."

Once again I told him no, that was OK. So I continued to wash load after load while my sons played the PS2 downstairs.

When we were upstairs, he told me we should get back together. We had been separated the last year and a half because he had had affair after affair. Cheating, cheating, and more cheating in my face. But we were still married.

"So can we get back together again?" he said.

I told him no. He asked me why. Just then my cell phone started ringing.

"Because your bitch is calling me right now, and she don't even block her caller ID. See?" I said. He looked down at the screen and recognized her number. "See, your bitch is calling me like we are patnas." I shook my head at him.

"You are hella crazy," he said to me.

"I sure am." I laughed out loud. "I sure love caller ID. She has been calling me and hanging up on me from blocked numbers for three years. Ten to fifteen times a day, every day, for three years. And now she doesn't even care to block her number."

We both laughed. Then he got really serious and looked in my eyes and said, "I'm so, so, so sorry. I'm sorry for everything I have ever done to you, and I'm sorry for putting you through so much. You have always had my back and have given me four beautiful kids. You always loved me, and you deserve the best, and I owe you and the kids. I apologize for everything I have ever done to you in your whole life."

I said, "Thank you." I was in shock, so I asked, "Why? Why did you say this?"

I had a strange feeling all day, and I couldn't figure out why. Auntie then came in and took some pics of him and me, then of him, me, and Nini, our youngest daughter. Then he went downstairs. I continued washing clothes. I must have had about seven or eight loads to wash, and he grabbed the basket from me, snatched it.

"Hey, give that back," I said.

"No. Why don't you let me help you finally?"

"Finally?" I asked.

A year and a half before, I had written down the date and time on a piece of paper and told him to put it in his wallet. He had asked me why. I had told him to just do it. That day I asked him to please go into his wallet and pull out that small piece of paper.

"I always wondered what that was for," he said.

"That was the last time I asked you to do anything for me, a year and a half ago," I said. Whenever I did ask, he would say that I nagged, nagged, and more nagged. So I didn't ask him to give the kids baths, wash clothes, grocery shop, do homework, and so on. I just did it, and it wasn't easy, because I was working and he wasn't.

"Wow!" he said. "I'm washing clothes. You go to bed. It's ten o'clock."

I was half-asleep, and I looked into the bathroom. He was washing and shaving his face and head. I went back to sleep.

My son was blowing up my phone. I answered.

"Mom, come pick me up." He had spent the night out, so his dad said he would pick him up. He left, and my husband and son went for a sandwich before heading back home.

I heard my husband say to our son, "Don't stay downstairs in the studio long." He had just sent up my younger son and cousin from playing the PS2.

My older son said, "I'm not."

My husband went back in the bathroom to finish shaving, then went back down to get the clothes out of the dryer, and came back upstairs.

12:04 a.m.

In my sleep, I thought I was hearing firecrackers, but It wasn't. Gunshots were what it was, coming from downstairs. I got up went to kitchen looked at the oven time, and it said 12:04 a.m.

I knew my son was downstairs. I couldn't find the house phone. My husband and I ran out of the house. It felt like a thousand hands around me, and I went back in the house, got my cell phone, and dialed 911.

I woke up all the kids and my aunt. I was screaming, "Wake up!" I went back downstairs, and my husband was running back up. He snatched me with both arms, locked the gate, and threw me down. The way he threw me down, I hit my head really hard on the kitchen tile. I hurt my head really badly, but that didn't matter. I could not believe my eyes.

I got up, and he walked toward me with both arms up. He was shot. He fell down to the floor and looked at me and my three children. My kids were in total shock. Their little eyeballs were popping out of their heads, and my oldest daughter was hysterical, completely hysterical.

I told her she was so brave and to let Daddy rest his head on her lap while I called 911.

Always have a landline; never call from a cell phone. They will put you on hold, transfer you to highway patrol, and then transfer you to 911 dispatch. So much of a waste of time. It took six to seven minutes just to do that. It seemed like forever.

While I was talking to my husband, I realized my eldest son hadn't come upstairs, and I didn't know if he was dead or alive. It's all that I kept thinking about. My heart was broken, but I kept my cool. So much was going on, and in the blink of an eye, my life had changed. I just wanted to ask God, why? Why?

Three of my children were crying as they watched their dad dying, and I was holding it all in, talking to him. After ten minutes, I called 911 again because there was no ambulance.

By then my aunt and I, plus the five kids, were going to carry him, but my son came upstairs. He was alive! He walked up to his dad, and his dad's eyes lit up. Monie was so happy. He rose up and gave him a thumbs-up, and my son ran out the door; he couldn't bear to watch.

My husband was on the floor. He wasn't bleeding a lot. We were telling him to hang in there. His friend was lying on the coffee table, shot in both legs. I was looking around, like, Wow, is this really happening? Three people shot: my son, his dad, and his dad's friend.

I was in total shock. I called his mom's house and said, "Get here fast, now! There's an emergency!" and hung up. I called twenty other family members and relayed the same message, all five-second calls: "Get to my house now!"

We were scared to move him. What if we killed him? Or hit his head on the concrete stairs? He was too heavy, 280 pounds. I called 911 for the third time, and I cursed that dispatch lady out so badly. I didn't mean to, but I was so furious. Where was the ambulance? It seemed it had been twenty minutes already.

I told my daughter she had to be a big girl and help Mom; her dad gave her a thumbs-up. I had to go outside and check up on my son. He had been shot twice in the buttocks, and the next-door neighbor helped him.

By now the police had come, and since I was outside, they wouldn't let me back in the house. All I could hear was my three kids crying, and the way the yellow tape was, I couldn't go in the house and I couldn't reach my son in front of me to help him.

I told the officer, "Look, my son is shot over there, and you won't let me over the yellow tape to help him, and my other three kids are over on the other side of the yellow tape, crying, and you won't let me cross that tape. My husband is in there, shot."

Finally, after explaining that to two or three officers, they let me back in the house.

Blood everywhere!

The ambulance finally arrived, but the paramedics said I couldn't ride with him. Come to find out, four people had been shot: my husband, my son, and two other people.

I was also hurt very badly from hitting my head against the tile. It almost knocked me out, but I didn't care about that. My main concern was my husband and son.

There were four ambulances, two fire trucks, and lots of police cars. It looked like a scene from a movie; this could not be real.

After my son went to the children's hospital and my husband went to Highland, my aunt, the kids, and I were questioned for an hour.

I said, "Look, you guys have to take this to the hospital. My son and husband have been shot. We need to go!" No one was arrested, no one knew a damn thing, and I got a call telling me to get to the hospital fast. After that call I told the officer I was advised that I needed to be at the hospital because it wasn't looking too good.

My aunt and cousin and a few other relatives went to the children's hospital to be with my son so I could go be with my husband, Monie.

My aunt and cousin would give me updates on my son, and the doctor called me and said, "Your son has been shot twice in the buttocks, and the reason he is alive is because he has fatty tissue. If he did not have the extra weight on him, he would have died. The two bullets got stuck in fat, basically." I was so happy to hear this news.

The doctor said, "He will be OK in three months. He needs to take meds twice a day and change his bandages three times a day, or he will get an infection, and he can die from it."

I said OK, no problem, I would make sure it was done. So he was discharged and came to Monie's hospital.

When I walked into the hospital, there were about twenty people already there. I was going to the main lobby, and while I was in the ER, the nurse called a patient, Margie Robinson, and my eyes got big. That was Monie's grandmother's name. She had passed away years ago, and I got spooked. Her name and his last name called. I got really scared but didn't tell anyone, because I didn't want to speak about death.

At the hospital, I found out another person in the studio had been shot, another friend of my husband's. Wow, four people.

As the hour went by, there were about forty of us, and after a couple of hours, there were a lot of people, family and friends. The doctor came up to me and said he was going to be in surgery for some hours.

My heart was racing, pounding. I was hella nervous. My nerves were a wreck. I had a headache; my stomach was turning. I was looking at my babies; they were so young. So little. My mind was so full, so scared. I was pacing around. I saw an *Awake* magazine on the counter. The article read, "Kids, do they understand death?" And I was begging God in my mind, please, God, don't let this happen! Please! I don't want to raise four kids alone; please, God, don't let him die. Please, he's too young. I am too young to be a widow. God, please! What am I going to do? What is my plan? I was telling myself to think positive.

I called my best friend Shugga, and I told her what happened.

She said, "Oh my gosh. Call me when he gets out of surgery." I informed her I would. She couldn't believe it. Then we did a big family prayer. I didn't cry; I didn't want to cry in front of my kids. I wanted to be strong, and I knew if I cried, they would also. So I was holding it all in the best way that I could.

I had just been talking to Monie a few hours before. We had been making plans to go to the mall the next day, and now he was on the operating table.

My dad left to go to work. He told me to call him when Monie was out of surgery.

While he was in surgery, we were waiting around, and I saw someone rush in with at least six boxes of blood, and I just felt it was for him.

Code Blue, Code Blue!

I saw the doctors and nurses running. I just knew in my heart he was dying, and after about twenty minutes, a doctor came up to me, a short white man—I forgot his name. He said with tears in his eyes, "Can I talk with you privately in a room?"

There were about fifty relatives in a big room, maybe even more. The doctor closed the door, and he said, "I'm sorry to say Mr. Robinson is no longer with us." All I could see was everyone screaming, crying, and going crazy. People were throwing things, crawling on the floor, cursing, some in shock.

Before the doctor made the announcement, I knew from the tears in his eyes that my husband was dead. The very first thought that crossed my mind was, how am I going to take care of four kids by myself? The second was, I can't believe it! I can't believe it. Where are my kids at? There were about a hundred or more people and relatives consoling my babies. How could I comfort all of them at once? My husband had two other children as well, and my stepdaughter was taking it hard.

Then two doctors came up to me and said, "We need you to identify the body." His parents wanted to, and I wanted them to as well. I really didn't want to; I was scared. I didn't want to believe it. But one of the doctors said, "No, you are his wife. I'm only letting you verify his identity." That's one of the hardest things I have ever had to do in my life.

I forgot to pray and ask God for help, but I know God was with me. I walked in, and he was on a table with a white sheet. There were one doctor and two police officers, and he was as big as a parachute balloon. They had given him so much blood.

"Do not touch him. You can look, but do not touch, or you will be asked to leave." His face and his body were totally swollen, but his arms and hands were normal. They gave me three or four minutes. I didn't make a sound, but I could hear myself screaming on the inside. I asked him in my mind, just yesterday you made plans to go to the mall with me, and now you are dead?

The officer asked me, "Is this your husband?"

"Yes," I replied.

"Is his name Jamonie Robinson?"

"Yes," I replied again. I just looked at all his tats, and he didn't look the same. I was numb!

"You are now done," the doctor said. "His body will be taken to the morgue. You can pick up his belongings there in a few days."

I looked at him and walked out. It was horrible to walk out and see his parents and my kids, knowing I had just confirmed that he was really gone and never coming back. Never! Shock, pure shock was on my brain.

I called my dad, and he asked, "How is he?"

"He's dead, Dad. He died."

My phone started ringing off the hook; his phone was ringing off the hook. When I answered my phone, I had to tell my family he was dead and then answer his phone and relay the same story hundreds of time. Major stress! It was overwhelming for me. A couple of females called too. I was nice and informed them that he had been killed that day.

There it was: my husband had been dead twenty minutes, and I had just confirmed his death. A chick that he used to talk to called my phone and asked, "Is it true? Is he really dead?" Wow! Talk about disrespectful.

I told her, "Yes, it is true, and don't call my phone again!" Show some kind of respect. Damn!

My husband's mom walked up to me and said, "You know I am going to help you with those kids, right?" It was like she read my mind, and then we hugged. That is Moms.

Auntie was heartbroken. There were so many people crying and screaming and yelling. All my kids were just so, so hurt. I wished I had eight arms so I could hug all my kids at the same time. I was in total shock and disbelief.

Bad news travels fast, and by now there were more than a hundred people at the hospital, and everyone was very upset. People were throwing and breaking things, and I couldn't take it anymore. It was too much for me.

My kids and I were tired and hungry. We had been up all night and day, so we left the hospital and the madness and rented a room at a hotel. Driving from the hospital with four kids, I realized I was thirty-one and a widow. My husband was dead, and everything was on me now!

As I was driving to the hotel, I was looking back at my babies in the rearview mirror. Two kids had their heads down. My heart broke, but I still didn't show them emotion. I wanted to scream, yell, punch someone, and cry my heart out. I was so sad, scared, and tired. So many mixed emotions.

My boyfriend from the eighth grade, whom I married and had four kids with, whom I had known since I was twelve, was gone, and I watched as he was dying and couldn't do anything. He was gone!

October 17, 2004

A year before, we had a talk about what would happen in the event of his death, a talk we had hundreds of times. He said, "If my AFNF [all family, no friends] don't take care of you, if my family don't take care of you, then nig**, hustle."

That convo came to my mind, and it was real; motherhood got real. My life got real, and I wasn't ready to deal with it or accept it, but yep, this was my life in high definition.

CHAPTER 7

October 17, 2005

"Love," by Musiq Soulchild, his favorite song...RIP, Monie Hogg

AT THE HOTEL I told a few very close family members where we were. I felt the need to be safe and protect my family. I didn't know whom to trust. I

had to plan a funeral on the day he was killed. I decided I had better get started.

My dad and aunt watched the kids and got them some food. I kept getting calls from the same chick who called me earlier at the hospital, so my mother-in-law took the phone and spoke to the girl and asked her to stop calling my phone; he was dead, and show some respect.

I took a shower to get ready to go to the funeral parlor and to take off the clothes that had Monie's blood on them. When I took a shower, as I was washing my hair, a lot of blood came from my head. I had really hit it hard, but I didn't care; I was alive and breathing and had four kids and a lot to do and plan. My son was in pain in the room, shot twice, and my husband was in the morgue. I couldn't have cared less about a busted head, but I really should have gotten checked too. But I just took the shower, closed my eyes, and cried. I could feel the weight on my shoulders, and it hadn't even been twenty-four hours yet.

We went to Sunset Memorial in Albany, California, and I picked out the casket with my mother- and father-in-law. We made all the arrangements, and we wanted the funeral to be within a week.

We then went to get flowers for the top of the casket and a flower stand. Swipe! $1,800 for flowers. Who knew it cost that much? I didn't, and I was learning a lot about planning a funeral.

While we were at the flower shop, the mortuary called, and they wanted their money within four days of the funeral. I went into a panic; I didn't have $19,000 for a funeral. I made a call, and a loving family member, Jimmy (forever our angel), FedX the check within two days. It was a big relief, and I was able to relieve some stress and use the rest of the money for other things I had to do.

So far we had gotten the wake and funeral planned on the same day that he was pronounced dead.

We went back to the hotel. My kids ate and watched TV, and then some of them cried themselves to sleep. It was so sad to watch this. I just got into bed and allowed them to cry on me.

The next day, we went to stay with my mother-in-law, Lillie. My mother-in-law and I are close; she's a second mom to me. We went to the house where the murder happened to get some pics for the obituary.

I put about a hundred pictures on the table. Myself, Auntie and Moms went downstairs to get more pictures, mainly my wedding pictures. But when we tried to go back upstairs, the door was locked, and when we opened it up, the hundred or so pictures were gone! They had disappeared into the sky. I guess Monie wanted them. I had no clue, so I had to repick pictures.

We got pictures together again; then we headed to the print shop to have the obituary done. The obituary was done on glossy paper, six pages, with pictures and writing on both sides. The print shop owner said in his forty years of business, Monie's obituary was the best he had ever done or seen, with the most pictures and the best front-picture design, like a magazine.

We ordered 1,500 obituaries, and I had to go back and order another 500 copies. It was very expensive, i had money in the bank to cover expenses. See, three months before, I had won a small lawsuit, and it came just in time. I used all the money on flowers, obituaries, and food for the repass; plus I got help from my dad and my husband's cousin Jimmy, and his best friend Will, so that was also very helpful.

Fifteen to twenty family members all pitched in to help with different things. I had been out of work for three months with no pay, and we also had gone to Colorado for a family reunion two months prior. By the time the money was gone, my disability pay kicked in, now I was the only breadwinner.

The family all made a trip together to Hilltop Mall, about fifteen of us. We went to get outfits for the wake and funeral, and my cousin Latosha helped me with the kids to find outfits.

Everybody else found stuff, but I couldn't really find anything, so my mother-in-law picked out an outfit for me, a really nice velvet pantsuit and a gray shirt. My sons and my brother and my cousin Jalil wore black suits, the same as Monie.

My sons picked out their daddy's suit for him and got fitted while I was shopping for my clothes. Before the wake and the funeral could happen, I had to go to the morgue to pick up my husband's belongings and pay for his body to be brought to the funeral home.

He had two rings, three twenty-dollar bills, and three two-dollar bills. Grandma always said carry a two-dollar bill in your wallet for good luck, and he had three of them. I put one in my wallet and gave one to my son and one to my mother-in-law. Looking at the money and rings, I saw they had Monie's blood on them.

I made twenty silver heart necklaces, with his picture engraved on them and our names on the back, to wear to the wake. They were very nice. The next day I went back and got another fifteen; so many people wanted one.

CHAPTER 8

The Wake

Saying good-bye is never easy, so I will say, "See you later"

BEFORE THE WAKE started, we left the mall, headed to the house, took showers, and got dressed an hour before everyone arrived at the wake.

I went in first for fifteen minutes with my dad, and Monie was in a casket. I looked at him, cried, screamed, and rolled all around the floor, over and over again. My dad gave me a big hug, and I screamed so much my voice was almost gone.

His mom came in. She was very strong; she held it together. My kids came in. My two younger kids were eight and six, so they cried, but my youngest didn't really understand. My eight-year-old son was the closest to his dad, and he and his brother took it the hardest until this very day.

My ten-year-old daughter, Ash, was hysterical, crying and crying to the point she was getting really sick and feeling faint. My oldest son was crying. I was looking at my family; it had fallen apart.

His family spoke at the wake, and his mom played a video of him at church when he was maybe four or five years old, preaching at church. I couldn't bear to watch the video. I raised my head to see in the casket, and the TV was next to him. I walked over to the casket and talked to him, and then a few other family members came over to the casket also. It was beginning to be too much for me. The whole week was, and then there were about twenty people surrounding me. I was looking at the casket, saying, "No, no, no." Next thing I knew, I passed out on the floor.

I had to leave after a few hours. I had to get ready for the funeral the next day. We told everyone good-bye, and everyone else was leaving as well. We headed out to feed the kids and go to the nail shop to get our nails done. We didn't have time to go to the hair shop.

The night of the funeral, I couldn't go to sleep. I watched my son Paris's rap video, which he had just made with his dad, at least four hundred times. I had it on replay to hear my husband's voice.

Moms told me I had to go to bed. Finally around three or four in the morning, I went to sleep and had a dream. My husband was sitting on the couch next to me. I was lying on his lap, and he was rubbing my head. He said, "When this comes to light, it will blow your mind." The dream ended.

Eleven years later, I have had about five or six dreams, but that dream was so real it was like he was actually sitting next to me.

Have no fear. Daddy's gone, Mommy's here.
Watching you take your last breath as your eyes talk to me.
Dying, gasping for breaths near death.
Mr. Grim Reaper crept.
It's a dark night; your body is taking flight.
You are going away; our four kids are watching you pass.
They can't believe their eyes. I can see shock;
I can hear cries; I can hear screams.
Daddy's gone, Mommy's here.
We can't believe it.
Is it a dream?
No, it's a murder scene.
Blood stinks; my heart sinks; my mind is racing.
The time is ticking; it's going by as you're passing away.
The ambulance hasn't found its way.
Hold on tight; don't close your eyes.
You're not going to die on me, not today.
Everything is going to be OK.

You do a thumbs-up to your baby girl.
You're leaving the world.
Daddy's gone, Mommy's here.
Daddy's gone, Mommy's here.
Watching you die, I'm helpless,
Wishing I was a doctor to save you,
But I know this isn't going to be the end of your
story.
I know when we get you out of surgery, every-
thing will be OK.
When the doctor said you were gone, the first
thing that crossed my mind,
How am I going to do this by myself? Daddy's gone,
Mommy's here.

CHAPTER 9

— ✂ —

Getting Ready for the Funeral

Don't forget to tell your favorite people you love them

Deliver me from my enemies, O my God, from
those rising up against me, may you protect me.

—Psalms 59:1

Never in a million years did I think my husband would be on a T-shirt, an RIP T-shirt. I always hated those shirts, always did, and someone has one on in front of me, it's like a dream to me.

I was looking for pictures for the obituary. Monie's friend had taken a picture of him in front of his Cougar, his favorite car, with cash everywhere on the ground with "RIP Monie Hogg the Great! Oakland's Finest" written across the picture. I told him, "I gotta have this. I want this picture for the front of the obituary."

He said OK. He had made some shirts with the same picture on it. Since the family wanted RIP shirts, I made some also with the same obituary cover.

Monie had given me $5,000, and I put it up in a sock and hid it in the mattress. Gone!

He had given me a bag of Baby Phat things, like high heels, shirts, jeans, earrings, a tennis bracelet, a purse, a necklace—all brand-new presents he got for our wedding anniversary, which was a month before his death. All items gone! I was beyond pissed. I remembered what store he went to, and I went back and rebought everything because it was special to me.

Certain clothes and personal items, all gone. All the money he had stacked up, gone. Guess somebody needed it more than I did. Man!

Visitors came over and helped themselves. All the money that I got from Monie was sixty-six dollars from his wallet given to me at the morgue: three twenty-dollar bills and three two-dollar bills. I ended up having to spend the sixty dollars on food for my kids. I still have a two-dollar bill in a special spot.

In my heart, I knew that all my faith would have to be in God, and he would provide, and I always prayed.

My dad really stepped up to the plate. He helped me buy new furniture for our new place. He also helped with food and rent. I told him as soon as I got some money, I would repay him.

The funeral was really big; about two thousand people came. I had the count from the sign-ins, and that's how many obituaries were made. Wow, he had a lot of love.

Everything came out beautifully; Pastor Humphery delivered his funeral at Olivet, and we had four retired police officers to feel safe. We had three limos; the kids and everyone looked really nice.

I gave advance notice to my husband's friends and cousins to please tell whomever not to come inside. I did not want to kick any female's ass; today was not the day. Please show me and my kids and family some kind of respect. Please.

I had two family members sit on the side of each of my four kids, just in case they needed comfort.

The flowers were beautiful, and Jamonie was in the suit his sons picked out. We had family speak, we read cards, and something got in me to speak. I never speak in large settings, but I mainly wanted to tell everyone thank you and also ask for peace, and that if anyone was family, I would need them to be there for my kids. Sitting in front of the casket was super hard, and then the casket opened, and we got to say our last good-byes. I gave him a kiss, and it was unbelievable!

We went to Sunset View and buried him. It was hard to see him go into the ground. We took group pictures, then headed to the repass.

The family helped with the repass with all kinds of food, and it was very nice. A few people that had too much to drink got on my nerves, so I left.

After the funeral there were hundreds of people outside the house where he was killed. There was a huge party, but I wasn't in the mood. I was tired and just disappointed that someone had destroyed my family. I stayed for a few minutes until a girl started talking crazy to me. I was about to unleash all my anger on her. But I left and went to Mom's house.

There were a lot of people there too. I ate, visited for a while, and then took three Advils and went into the big closet with a pillow and blanket and closed the door and cried myself to sleep. Today was over, and I was glad. RIP, Monie.

CHAPTER 10

— ❧ —

Life Changes

In the blink of an eye, life will change
Life changes…
Life changes…

MY WHOLE LIFE changed. Year 2005. I was in a new house; I rented my uncle Jose and auntie Wendy's home. They let me move in without a deposit; what a blessing! The whole house was brand new: new furniture, new city, new start. But we hadn't been in our new home for even a month when two guys decided to pull into our driveway and start burning rubber, which really scared my kids.

I said to myself, "I am going to buy a house and move out of the Bay ASAP."

So I started to search and search for places. Two years before Monie was killed, I was really paying bills and fixing my credit so I could buy a home. I couldn't find a house under $300,000 that wasn't in the ghetto or in a very bad neighborhood. I finally found a house an hour and a half away from Oakland.

I had it custom built, four bedrooms, living room, dining room, kitchen, three bathrooms, washroom, garage, and backyard, an upstairs and downstairs home with all stainless steel kitchen appliances. I got a bank loan approved a first and second on a $410,000 house with $10,000 down, and the builder gave a $5,000-down incentive.

The house took four months to build. I drove to the title company to sign paperwork. Before I did, I called my job and asked for a transfer. I had put my request in four months prior. My manager informed me that it was approved, so I was like, OK. I signed my John Hancock.

I was now a widow with four kids, but I had a great job, I had just bought a brand-new home in a brand-new development, brand-new furniture, and a brand-new Tahoe truck. I had fixed my credit so good I took my minivan and traded it in for a brand-new SUV using my job discount without having to put a dollar down.

So in one month, between a $410,000 home and a $40,000 car, I was making big life changes all by myself and feeling confident that I could do anything even though I was a widow with four kids. I was in a brand-new city, and my life was changing fast.

Three days after I bought my house, my manager changed her mind and didn't transfer my job. I began to start a three-year commute. Driving back and forth was very stressful and very expensive. So to save on gas, I stayed at my mom's house two or three days out of the week. I had XM satellite radio and OnStar, and I loved the new car, but I hated that it was a gas guzzler. I spent at least $1,000 to $1,200 a month on gas, or even more.

I worked in Oakland. My kids went to school out there, so I had a one-and-a-half-hour commute, but when we got home, it was great! I bought a sixty-inch flat-screen TV and put it on the wall with speakers, and we just stayed home, watched movies, and blasted music. Four bedrooms, three baths, upstairs and downstairs, garage—life was great!

Every Sunday I barbecued. My kids and my niece KK and nephew Doodah would party every weekend. I'd make cupcakes, greens, cornbread, baked beans, macaroni and cheese, links, hotdogs, chicken, steaks, and peach cobbler. I would make enough for two days; then Tuesday we would have tacos or spaghetti.

We lived on Round Table pizza Fridays. I would order it from the road twenty minutes before we got off the exit. I would go to the store, get gas, stop and get money out of the bank, and then pick up the pizza. The same routine every Friday. I would then take the kids to get clothes at the house to go to Grandma's; meanwhile I would have a piece of pizza in my hand while driving.

Friday was my night to go to the casino, every Friday. After dropping the kids off, I would go home, jump in the shower, put on a velour sweat suit, get in my truck, and take a thirty-minute drive to the casino. My plan? Win money, money, money. Half the time I would lose; the other half I would win, and win big.

One Friday night I took $750 to the casino. I took $700 into the casino and left $50 along with my ATM card in the car. I lost $700 in about three hours, losing and winning. Then I lost all $700. I ran back to my car to get the $50 and ran back inside to the same machine.

I lost $48 of it, and I was like, damn, I have to use my ATM card if I want some fries and a milkshake from Fat Burgers, because I am going to scream! I had taken out $3,000 from my 401(k), and that was my Friday money to gamble, so I could flip that money for my gas, food, and mortgage.

I was feeling sick as hell. There was $2 left on the screen; I had just lost $748. I pushed the button. I hit for $12,000; I was hecka happy!

I got up and cashed out and went home, bumping my music, checking my rearview, me, my music, and my little friend, my .38. I was hella happy!

The next day I went back to the casino and brought $500 with me and hit for $7,000, and ten minutes later I hit again for $7,000. In two days I had made $26,000. I cashed out and took a vacation week off. I was going to pay bills, buy groceries, give the family money, and hit the mall. I took the kids to breakfast and the movies, Jamba Juice, Starbucks, the mall, McDonald's, and Baskin-Robbins. We had a ball. I paid my utilities and my cell phone bill for a year. I bought Safeway gift cards and put them up for my food and gas so if I ever went broke, I would have a fall-back plan of $3,000 left in gift cards. I paid my mortgage for two months and then went back to work and my Friday hustle.

When you go to the casino four times a month, you may see a few of the same people, and I always saw this same older Chinese man in the "baller" section. I would sit next to him. He was about seventy years old, and he brought me good luck. He would always say, "Follow my lead." I always would win nothing under $3,000. I really didn't play cards well, so he was my teacher.

I was getting used to having money from the casino, so I stayed in the mall, and next thing you know, my dining room just had bags and bags of new stuff.

My mom said, "You be shopping too much. You have a shopping problem."

I told her, "I'm winning money, working, taking care of kids, and my 401(k) is doing well, and I'm getting fat commission checks, so I'm having a little fun for a moment, but for the most part, I never shop anymore."

It was just bills, gas, mortgage, cell phone bills, and the kids' wants and needs. So I just had fun for a few months, and it would be a long time before I shopped again.

Life was all about the kids, school, homework, work, commuting, and taking care of us. Bills, cooking, and cleaning. Some days I had time for a movie, but most days I was beat and really didn't go out and do adult stuff with my friends all the time, because I was tired.

I didn't realize just how much of a load a single mom has to carry by herself, and I was learning the true meaning of it.

"Life changes" is an understatement.

CHAPTER 11

Stolen Love

Steal, verb
Definition
1. Take without permission

I WAS FIFTEEN years old. I was supposed to go straight home, but I didn't. I wanted to go visit my friend; he used to be my boyfriend. I already knew the rules, but this time I would beat the streetlights and make it home. I gave my friend a hug and went inside.

We talked, watched TV, kissed a few times, and hugged. Then he said, "Let's have sex." I told him no.

As I was looking for a way out, I realized his windows all had bars on them. He was chasing me all around his home, which was very small. We did this for about forty-five minutes.

I was getting tired, he was getting tired, and he was starting to get really angry. He threw me into the wall, and I hit my head. I was thinking, you didn't listen to your parents. Now look.

He was my friend; how could he do this?

His front door was one of those doors that you couldn't get in or out of without a key. He told me, "You can't leave. Do you see the door and the bars?"

His house phone rang; it was his aunt.

I began to scream, "Let me out of here. Let me out of here," over and over again. I could hear her say, "What's going on?"

That phone call made him unlock the door, and I ran home twenty-five blocks. I left my shoes, and I ran home so fast with tears running down my face.

Close call.

I got busted outside by my aunt. She gave me that look and walked in the house with me. Needless to say, the streetlights had just come on, and I was on a month's punishment, but I didn't give a damn. I was happy to be confined to my bedroom, which I nicknamed San Quentin.

The First Time

I was nineteen years old. My firstborn, my son, was about one year old. On that day I had been cleaning up the house and washing clothes. I was running low on diapers, but I really didn't feel like going to the store, so I let it get later and later.

My car wasn't working, so I called around to look for a ride, but no one was able to pick me up and take me. It was after nine o'clock, and the store down the street was already closed.

So my neighbor said he would give me a ride. I had known him for about eight years, and he was cool. He had tried to talk to me for the last four or five years, but I would always turn him down and remind him that I had a boyfriend. He would always see us together. I knew he had twins on the way and a girlfriend that knew who I was, so I didn't think that anything would come of that night.

I got into the car with him. The plan was to go to the grocery store and get diapers. I gave him ten bucks for gas. I had left my son with my sister, so I told the guy I needed to get right back. We went to Eastmont Mall, and I went in to get diapers. I purchased diapers and got back in the car. I thanked him, and we took off.

On the way back home, I noticed he wasn't going in the right direction. I asked him where he was going. He said, "Oh, we are going to the movies." He was headed to the drive-in movies at the coliseum.

I told him, "No. You are taking me home; my sister has my son."

He proceeded to tell me, "No, we are going to the movies."

I was hot! Very upset. So upset I started to sweat. I started to panic, and I got scared; I said a silent prayer.

He took out his handgun and put it in his lap. My eyes got big!

He started talking. "I've been trying to talk to you for four years, and now you need me for diapers, huh?"

He took out a condom. As he was putting the condom on, I was thinking, Trinese, you did this to yourself. You did! If you had been more responsible, you would not be in this situation.

He put the gun to my head and told me to take my pants off. He then climbed on top of me in the passenger seat and put the gun back to my head.

I was disgusted and wanted to vomit as he kissed me, but I was scared to move. My eyes looked up to the gun, and the clip was in it. I wanted it to be over, but it was what seemed like the longest twenty minutes of my life in that car. When he was finished, he said, "OK, we are done. It wasn't that bad. Now you can go home."

I closed my eyes and put my head down as he dropped me off at home.

When I got home, it was maybe two hours later, and my sister was upset. "You knew you didn't have any diapers left. What took so long?" she said.

Then she looked at me and asked, "What happened to you?" My hair and clothes were messy, and my face looked like I had been crying.

I told her, "I got raped. Do not tell anyone."

She gave me a hug. I changed my son's diaper and jumped in the shower. The next morning my neighbor knocked on my window and said, "Hey, you better not tell anyone," and walked away.

I got dressed and knocked on his door.

When he answered, I said, "Hey, I don't know if I'm going to the police. I don't know if I'm going to tell my dad, my uncle, or my cousins. I don't know if I'm going to tell my boyfriend and his friends. I don't know if I'm going to knock on your door one day and blow your head off. I don't know if I will do that to your girlfriend. But what I do know is that you better move, because I don't know which one I am going to do."

Of course I was all talk. But his ass moved with the quickness, and I never saw him again.

Rape: Stolen Love Part 2

It was 2006, Valentine's Day. I woke up and decided I was going to buy about ten family members really nice presents from Macy's and several different stores, and we would have a Valentine's Day party. So I told my kids and family about it, got up, and got dressed.

First I went to get coffee; then I went to my husband's grave and put some flowers on it. Feeling sad and depressed leaving, I would always go to my husband's grave to scream and cry since it was in the hills, and it was my way to relieve stress.

I got the car washed, and then I went to Macy's and started my shopping. I spent about $5,000 on gifts. I was getting calls from blocked numbers playing on the phone. "I'm going to do something to you" (laughter in the background). The calls kept coming and coming. It started to really get to me, so I screamed, yelled, and cursed them out, and then I turned my phone off.

I stopped by my mom's house first and gave her some really nice boots. I visited with my mom for about four or five minutes. I went back outside, and all the stuff I just bought, gone! Taken. I had forgotten to lock the door. Man! I was so upset. I was on my way to drop the stuff off to my kids and other relatives. They took about 80 percent of the things I bought. So I went to my aunt's to explain what happened to everyone and took some things over to my kids.

Later on in the day, I don't know why, but all of a sudden, I got really sad, lonely, and depressed, so I went to my other aunt's house and vented by yelling at six relatives about different things I was upset about. It was really random and out of the blue, shocking for them to see me yell and be very upset.

So my mom and aunt called the police and put me on a 5150 watch. Interesting how some people can cuss, yell, and vent all the time, but the minute that I do it, I'm crazy. What I should have done on Valentine's Day was book a flight to Hawaii and have a tropical drink.

But no, instead I vented, and it was a very bad idea that cost me big. As I was walking to the ambulance, my head was down, and I was sad. They hooked the IV up and gave me relaxing meds.

The first place they took me to was John George. Can you say scared to death! Scared! It reminded me of a horror movie, so I told the director I needed to be out of there in the next hour to a better hospital. I was sad, lonely, and depressed, not mentally gone. So if she didn't get me the hell out of that place, I was going to sue them.

She had me moved to another hospital within thirty minutes. As I walked in, a seven-foot, at-least-450-pound man, literally a lumberjack, got me out of the ambulance and walked me in. I held his arm tight.

The workers laughed and said, "We have never seen anyone hold on to him. They usually run. Why are you holding his arm?"

I said, "Because he is big and I feel safe, and if anyone messes with me, he can knock them out."

They all laughed so hard and said, "You're right and have too much damn sense."

I had never been to a mental institution before. Walking in, I saw both men and women. As I got booked in, I started my menstrual, and I was just like, wow! What a day, and man, how it was ending. I said to myself, "God must not love me."

So I decided that I wasn't going to care anymore. After I was in the hospital for about three or four days, they explained that I was on a thirty-day hold on a 5150. I knew if no one paid my bills and I didn't work, I would lose the brand-new home I had had for about two years, and my credit would be affected.

My job was trying to fire me through catch-22s of disability paperwork. I couldn't turn in paperwork if I was in the hospital, literally locked up. My kids came to visit me. I was so hurt and ashamed of myself I could barely look at them. I love my kids.

I had my sister get my purse and wrote her a check to take care of bills and my kids. After about a week, I just gave up and went to an empty room and lay in there for a few days, and all of a sudden, I felt a lot of hands all over me.

There were about ten patients praying over me, and I started screaming, "Get the f*** away from me." They told two nurses, and the nurses opened the window, put me in a wheelchair, and then took me to the bathroom that had an open shower.

They cut my clothes off, gave me a shower, did my hair, put lotion on me, brushed my teeth, and dressed me. Then they wheeled me to the cafeteria area. All the patients who had prayed over me looked at me. I wasn't really eating, and I would spit the meds out, and they had cameras.

This young black guy, about twenty-eight or thirty years old, whispered in my ear, "You need to ask them how long they have been here. You better start taking showers every day, eating, and you better start going to classes. You better get it together, or you will be here forever. Ask them! Get it together now!"

So I asked a couple of people how long they had been there. One man said two years, one lady had a year with five more months to go (they kept adding time), and another lady had thirty days, now six months.

I spoke with the doctor, and he said he might add more time since he didn't see improvement. I started going to 90 percent of my classes, taking a shower morning and night, washing my clothes, eating, wearing new clothes, and even taking the medication, which made me extremely sleepy and slow.

Meanwhile this guy kept trying to talk to me. Now the staff thought he spoke no English, but every time he sat next to me, he spoke English, but when he was around the staff, he acted like he knew no English. The guy kept looking at me every meal, and that's why I was scared to take showers, because there weren't any locks on the door, so anyone could walk in.

I asked my brother to bring me ten bars of Ivory soap and the longest socks that he could find when he came back the next day. So he did. Before I went to bed, I took the ten bars of soap and put them inside the sock, wrapped the sock around my arm, and placed it under my pillow as a weapon.

Later that night, as I was sleeping, the guy came into my room and tried to get in bed with me. I immediately attacked him with the ten bars of soap in the sock. I was hitting him over his head, in his face, and he was screaming. He then ran to the staff and said that I attacked him.

Instead of them asking me what happened or why he was in my room—trying to rape me—they came in and sedated me, and I fell fast asleep.

When I woke up, I felt like I had had sex, and my whole body was sore. I knew he had come back in my room.

As we ate breakfast, the guy made it a point to sit across from me, shake his head up, and say, "Yeah, I did it, and it's done."

I should have sued, I should have pressed charges, but what I did was go to the doctor's office and tell him, "Thanksgiving is tomorrow, and it's also my husband's birthday. My kids need me. I did everything that you requested. On top of that, I got raped, and your staff made it possible." I explained what took place. I said that I had better be released tomorrow, or guess who was getting sued. And then I walked out.

My aunts came to visit me. The same doctor went to the bathroom, then went to the cafeteria and came back with my plate. He said that he wanted to watch me eat! The food was chili, and I could smell that he put something in it. So I told him I would let him watch me eat, but I wanted a different plate. I sent my aunt to get another plate and ate it and told him he could eat the one he brought.

The next day he released me, and I didn't sue or press charges as I should have.

Stolen love.

PS. Dear reader! If you are reading this chapter and you have been raped, trust me, I know the feeling, and God pulled us through! You, yes you! You are awesome! You are beautiful! You are loved! You are power-ful, and you for certain are God's beautiful creation! You are strong!

Love you, my sistas. In the process of life, it keeps going. Don't forget to love yourself (you-only days).

It's very important to love you, especially in a time of stolen love.

We have to build ourselves back up!

I hope this helps someone. Love and hugs!

CHAPTER 12

— ✂ —

Depression and Suicide

May your troubles be less and your blessings be more and nothing but happiness come through your door

DEPRESSION AND SUICIDE—THOSE two words are real words that affect lives. If you know any family members or friends who are down and out, uplift them, pray with them, check on them, and talk with them; it's so important.

Sometimes people don't show just how depressed they really are, but if you know a person has been beat up in life, that's the clue.

When I was young, I didn't know what depression was until my grandmother was murdered and my mom became depressed, and I was too. I gained a lot of weight and then got teased about it and then lost a lot of weight.

Then my sister getting cancer took a toll. I was so unhappy to see my sister go through everything she had to endure.

There were two times I was actually going to try to commit suicide, and thank God I prayed before I took action.

One day my kids were acting up, and they were all pretty young in age, and I was having a bad day, and I said a prayer. I said, "God, send someone to save me." And a few minutes later, my mom knocked on the door and said, "Go to the nail shop and take a break. I'm gonna take the kids, and they can spend the night."

I packed the kids' bags, and they left with my mom. I went to the nail shop, and when I left, I felt much better and a little happy and thankful. I just had a bad day that got better. I was so glad God sent my mom!

The second time, I felt like everything was literally falling apart and I had a brick backpack on my shoulders. Nothing was going right. I was about to lose my house, my credit, and the money invested in my house, and I gave up, thinking I didn't have any options. I was thinking of ways to end my life; it's crazy how I was so over all life's problems.

Throughout the day, my baby girl Nini, who was about ten years old, was following me around the house all day. "Hey, Mom, let's watch a movie. Let's watch another movie, Mom. Hey, Mom? Order a pizza." All day she was by my side, my angel.

So I said, "After the movie, you are going to Grandma's house."

Now I was by myself, with the kids at Grandma's. I decided I was going to get my handgun and use it. I was just about to leave, and I said a prayer. I said, "God, if you really love me, you will send someone right now, because I'm gonna blow my head off." That was my prayer.

Less than one minute later, my mother-in-law and father-in-law came walking up to my car, and she put her finger to my head and said, "God told me to tell you he loves you. You should come by the house. I made tacos."

I said OK.

I put my head down and cried and thanked God. I decided I would never take my life for granted, ever!

I ended up losing my house, car, credit, and money, and it was depressing, but I got to start off fresh, and material things come and go.

You can have everything, everything, but if you don't have God, joy, happiness, and health, material things mean nothing compared to that.

I began to search for happiness, and I started praying more, playing music, walking by the lake, reading, and spending time with my kids and nieces and nephew. Seeing them happy made me happy. I love to cook, so on Saturdays and Sundays, I would really cook a lot of food and watch movies.

When you focus on all your problems in life, it will weigh you down. Focus on the good things, and handle one problem at a time. Try to fix everyone's problems and add your problems, and it spells a disaster waiting to happen.

Live in the moment, on purpose. Looking back on the past, especially living in the past—part of depression is not letting go.

Living for the now, so many things I took for granted, and I wasted lots of time being depressed and not being more positive and looking at the brighter side.

When you're told you may die soon (not that the doctors know exactly when), that's when you want to start living, and my brain started to race, and it was thinking, "I have so much to do."

I had never seen a psychiatrist before, so after my husband was killed, I took my mom's advice and went. Man, after talking with the doctor for about twenty minutes, he didn't believe half of what I was saying. He said I needed to bring him proof.

I laughed and said, "Take ten minutes and look at my medical record, and it will show you. My husband was murdered, and both my sons have been shot two times each."

After he did, he said, "I'm sorry. Wow, your life is a war, and I don't know how you have survived! And you have to save yourself. Leave the kids alone and go somewhere, and just survive."

I didn't like what he said. I said, "They are minors, and I love my kids." It was good talking the problems out, but I felt it didn't solve them.

The home invasion didn't really hit my brain until a year later. I stayed extremely busy, but when posttraumatic stress syndrome hits, it does not ask permission. I kept having instant replays of my husband in the back of the ambulance, over and over.

I hardly slept, and I hardly ate. Over a few months' time, I lost sixty pounds; I went from a size 14 to a size 4. I didn't trust very many people, and I stayed to myself. I was a sinking ship, and depression was the Titanic.

After about nine months, one night before I went to bed, I asked God to please help me out the darkness and wipe my brain of depression. I woke up feeling so much better. I started to get rest and eat good food and really focus on not being depressed, and it worked.

I had a moment a few months ago when I was re diagnosed for the fourth time; I was so devastated to hear I had cancer again, for the fourth time in a row, for the fourth year. It was like a car crashed and I was in it, and my brain didn't want to hear that.

Chemo again! Hell no, heck no, no, thank you! I cried every day for a month. I lost twenty-seven pounds and just stayed in my room. Then finally I couldn't cry anymore, and I was ready to be a big girl. Ready to get it all over with, again.

Yep, that's how life is sometimes. You gotta roll with the punches. Even if you have to always fight, it seems.

Having cancer showed me who had my back. I was down to see a couple of people I thought would be there, and they were not. I broke my neck for them, and they didn't for me. I learned not to get down and upset by that, and God did place so many angels in my life to pull me through, and I'm thankful for that.

My manager Elo put together fund raisers at my job with my team. They sold food and snacks on payday, and they helped me when I was really down each year I had cancer. My kids would always say, "We hope we get a job with such caring people." They were really impressed!

I will never forget that when you're down, always know there's somebody who loves and cares for you, and it's always good to reach out to them. They may not know what's going on with you either.

When we had the home invasion, I was asleep, and if you are wakened out of your sleep in the middle of night by something like that, it takes a very long time to trust going to sleep, and sleep is very important.

No sleep, with not eating a lot, combined with fear and anxiety, stress, and worry, with paranoia, plus posttraumatic stress syndrome, add having hardly any trust for anyone—it took a lot of years for me to learn how to let go of the past and to forgive people who caused me pain and not to worry and to build a closer relationship with God. Slowly I was back to my old self, and I healed more by making an effort to change myself and my attitude and learning how to be more positive in negative situations.

The main thing that pulled me out of depression was God first and my family and friends. I can't thank them enough, especially my kids. They have been through a lot, just like me, and weathered the storms.

You do get stronger with all the battles, and you look back and say, "Wow, I made it through!"

I know it's not easy, and I know someone is reading my story, and your story may be worse than mine. Just don't lose hope and faith or give up! All we can do is the best we can. Always know you have someone who loves you and cares.

One day at a time. Breathe. Baby steps.

With everything I'm going through and have been through, I'm counting my blessings, and I have a lot to be thankful for. Wishing you the best! We are too blessed to be stressed. Hugs.

If anyone needs help, call the National Suicide Prevention Lifeline, 1-800-273-8255. Much love and God bless.

CHAPTER 13

Gun Violence

Why can't we live in peace…instead of resting in peace?
Where is the love?

GUN VIOLENCE IS the norm today. Each week there's something new, and it's just so mind blowing that this is what is going on in the world. Wow, kids killing kids like it's nothing. It's crazy.

One day I didn't get a ride from my mom after school, so my best friend and I got a ride from her boyfriend. There were four of us. I was in the back seat, and her boyfriend's patna was in the back with me. I told them drop me off home first. Twenty minutes later, the car got shot up, and my BF and the guy in the back seat were killed. That day I wanted to beat the streetlights for some reason, and it saved my life.

I have had a gun pulled on me a few times, and it's very scary, very! The first time I was on my way to get gas, ice cream, and a cheesesteak; that's all I planned. So I got gas, ordered the cheesesteak, and got the ice cream. I was only about twenty years old. I was bumping my music, eating french fries, and I was passing a fry to my one-year-old son. My window was down, and I had my head turned to my son.

Next thing you know, I was involved in an attempted carjacking. The gun was at my head! He said, "Don't move! Get out the car! And don't worry about your son."

I was in total shock, but I hit the pedal so hard and burned rubber out of the parking lot. Close call! So happy we got out of that situation in one piece!

The second time a gun was pulled on me, I was with my son again. Lil Monie wasn't even two years old yet, and we had another bad situation. We had just left my little adopted sis Brandi's house; she had had a baby shower. I caught a cab to the train. As I was getting out of the cab, a man passed by the cab. I didn't notice that he came around the cab. Next thing you know, I had a gun placed in my back.

The man shouted, "Give me your jewelry!" I was handing the cab driver money at the time. He saw me getting robbed, and he tried to drive off. Mind you, half my body was in the car, and my son was in his car seat. All this while a gun was placed in my back. I gave the necklaces to the guy quickly, and he ran off. I got my son's car seat out, and the cab sped off.

I was so grateful to God to be alive! I also started having trust issues with people, especially if I didn't know them.

The third time was when I was raped by my neighbor and he had a gun to my head. I'm so glad I'm able to even be here to write this book. I have been through quite a few close call situations. God is good!

You never know who you may encounter and what they have planned with a gun. Always pray for God to protect you!

Who knew that gun violence would change my life totally? Guns and bullets. With my boyfriend and my best friend Keisha being murdered in Oakland, I had a lot of sorrow from losing two close people to me, but when my grandmother was murdered, that really affected me. I could not believe it and didn't want to either! We were really close, and all I had left were memories.

When you have fatherless children, Father's Day is not a liked day. Lots of tears for my children. And visits to his gravesite to place flowers on his birthday are never fun, but that's my life. Our lives have changed.

And that's life. People make decisions, and other people have to live with them. When something bad happens, what are the top two things people say? "Everything happens for a reason" and "I'ma pray for you." When you are mad at the world, when bad things happen or you lose someone, sometimes you don't want to hear something positive, even though that's actually exactly what you need, someone positive in your ear. When you're standing in a dark place, get to the light quick!

With the impact of my grandmother and my husband killed, a home invasion, me playing nurse to three of the four gunshot victims, including my thirteen-year-old son, what I will never forget is dire shock in my husband's and children's eyes. Sometimes when ambulances pass me by, I can flashback to see him for the last time in the back of ambulance. It's crazy what the mind stores!

Hey, it's springtime, spring break. The kids were out of school. I was dropping my son off in a neighborhood I hate. I was fussing at him, and I said, "You don't need to be down here."

"It's good, Mom," he said.

I went home with a very bad migraine; I had a bad feeling. An hour later he was shot. He had already been shot with his dad. I got the call and rushed to Highland. He was walking in the wrong place at the wrong time; it was a drive-by. He survived but left Highland the next day. He didn't want to be at the same place where his dad died, and I don't blame him. Thankful and thousands of prayers.

Next year, during spring break, can't catch a damn break, it seems.

My younger son loved his dad. He had a very special relationship with his dad, and he took it maybe the worst. Well, all my kids took their dad's death very hard, but my sons took it extremely hard. For about two years, my son P would wear his father's RIP T-shirt to school every day. Sometimes, I would have to cut the shirt off him while he slept, and he would put a new one on.

So anyway, a classmate made fun of his dad being dead, and they argued and argued, and one day the classmate shot him coming off the bus. Yes, he shot him in the back, and the bullet traveled through his heart loop; then he shot him in the chest, and the bullet traveled through his lung.

Let me tell you how that day went. At lunch I had a very bad migraine, and I got a sharp, sick feeling like something very bad was going to happen. I stopped in the middle of the street and prayed as I crossed the crosswalk, "Please, God, protect my sons. Please, God. Amen!"

As soon as I was off work, I got a call that P was missing and everyone was looking for him. I left work. My boyfriend was in the car, waiting to pick me up, and I told him, "Let's go down and look for him not too far away." So we were circling blocks, and I saw a body on the ground a few blocks away, but I didn't think that was my son. No, I didn't, but fifteen minutes later I got the call. It was the children's hospital. My son was in surgery, and the nurse said he had whispered my number. "Come quickly."

From the damage done, he was blessed. The bullet went through his heart instead of breaking apart his heart like his dad's, but the damage to his lung, chest, and back put him on life support for eight days, and I was scared to death! There was a 50/50 chance of survival once he was taken off life support. Before they took him off, the doctors warned me. I just sat there and sobbed, and on top of all that, my sister had just had surgery and her second chemo for breast cancer, and my car had broken down the week before, so yeah, life was kicking my butt real good! I was a wreck!

I never cried so much in my life, but with my son on life support, man, I didn't want to lose him, so I prayed and prayed. I begged and begged God to please save my son!

My son was placed in a high-priority secure area, and they let only his grandparents and me visit, but in the intensive care unit, there were about fifteen patients in this locked area. My son's neighbor, a baby, was on life support, but she wasn't going to make it. It was so sad. So this baby had hundreds of visits, visitors saying a last good-bye, and it turned out so many people that visited the baby knew my son, and it was all bad. His friends would pass by and see him and go crazy, and it just so happened my daughter was friends with the baby's mother, and when she saw her brother, she lost it. Super stressful!

Eight days, and it was time to take him off life support. When he was taken off life support, the first thing he said was, "Mom, I wanna get out of here!" My dad and I laughed; he was his ole grumpy self again, thank God!

He made it through! God is great! Almost three months in the hospital and three months at home being his nurse, so six months playing his nurse, wasn't easy at all. Kids, man, kids, but a mother's love.

I love my kids, period. A mother's love is unconditional and forever!

My son's best friend was killed a few weeks ago, and he was devastated. He had been hanging with him for about ten years. And unfortunately, so many kids are dying left and right. I always think what can be done to change this.

So I personally talk to all my kids' friends, even if I think my kids and their friends are not going to listen me! I plant the seed over and over and over again. "Hey, you're going the wrong way. Hey, get a job, a business. Go to school. Do something positive." I have said it a hundred times and a thousand times over to many kids and my own.

If no one stays on these kids, the gun violence will only get worse. It's so sad to see all these RIP posts on social media daily.

And yes, I do believe that we have to pray for them, because these kids today don't listen, and they can be very disrespectful, and you do reap what you sow. But some kids can change with the right people backing them. Sometimes when you hear someone on you about stuff, it promotes change.

These kids are looking for love as well and getting it from all the wrong places.

I pray that we all can reach out and be a mentor to just one young person, and maybe we can see some changes, spread love and peace.

—— ✂ ——

CHAPTER 14

Momma Nese's Relationship Tips

"Real Love," by Mary J. Blige

Rule #1

LOVE GOD FIRST! Love yourself second. God will put that perfect someone in your life that's just for you.

Rule #2

Always be number one. Refer back to rule #1, and everybody knows that. And if you don't buy a clue, don't be a fool; you are smarter than that. That's something I learned along the way. I don't want to share my man, period!

Rule #3

If you have to chase him or force him to stay, two words: bye-bye, baby! And tell her I said hi.

If someone you love doesn't love you, why are you wasting your tears? That person doesn't care. Why should you care about someone who cares nothing for you?

If there were a free gas station, wouldn't you be there every day? Don't give your love away for free; you are worth more than that.

Rule #4
Keep it fun& spicy!!

Rule #5
Love yourself now, every day!

Rule #6
If he keeps doing the same thing time and time again, and you allow him to treat you that way, he always will!

Rule #7
If he says he's going to marry you and keeps saying it every year without making the effort, stop wasting your time with that loser. Bye.

Rule #8
Ladies, get someone that loves and respects you, someone loyal that you can be happy with!

Rule #9
Get someone you can trust! This is so important. Someone who would never hurt you and who guards your heart.

Rule #10
You should be happy; love should make you happy, so very happy. When you have love in your heart, nothing tops that feeling.

Yep, these are all lessons I had to learn, but the hard way.

You have to learn the rules of the game, and you have to play better than anyone else.

—ALBERT EINSTEIN

CHAPTER 15

— ⚮ —

The Topic Is Love

*Love is patient. Love is kind. It does not envy.
It does not boast. It's not rude. It is not self-
seeking. It is not easily angered. It keeps no
record of wrong. Love does not delight in evil, but
rejoices with the truth. It always protects. Always
trusts. Always hopes. Always perseveres.*

—CORINTHIANS 13:4–7

LOVE—THAT WORD WILL get you every time, I tell you. What's love got to do with it? Exactly.

I love strawberry cheesecake, Round Table pizza, BBQ, garlic noodles, and garlic buttery crab with an apple martini. I love apple pie with vanilla ice cream, red velvet cake, Baskin-Robbins pralines 'n' cream, mac 'n' cheese, and soul food. Fried chicken, Wing Stop lemon pepper wings, gumbo, and some good cereal at midnight every blue moon.

OK, I love food. Now that we got that out of the way…

When love hurts my feelings, two scoops of ice cream make me feel better. Yeah, I'm crazy, the good crazy. You love me!

My first little puppy love was our little puppy Buffy. He was so cute, but he went to sleep in a pothole and got run over. We were heartbroken, my little sister and I. That's when I first understood a little bit how my heart worked.

My first real little puppy love, my first little boyfriend, I'll call Young B. He was cute and shy, and I was shy. I liked him a lot in elementary school. He played basketball and baseball. We kissed a couple of times and held hands and talked on the phone. Too cute.

But one day, I overheard his sister say, "Hey, you are liking this girl, and you need to be focused on baseball."

He was only eleven years old, but I saw star potential in him, like I knew, I had this feeling, he was going to make it, and he did. He went on to play professional baseball. Because I overheard what his sister said, I broke up with him, because she was right. Some girls probably would never have tripped off someone's future, but I made the right choice. It was all love, little puppy love, that is.

When I was in junior high school, I loved to write poems. I was going to be a writer, I said.

I loved Big Daddy Kane, Al B. Sure, and Michael Jackson. You couldn't tell me Michael was not my boyfriend. Everybody loved MJ, period.

Listen, my parents were strict. The room I shared with my sister was nicknamed San Quentin, so love was definitely out of the question at the house. And of course having any boyfriends was not allowed until we were eighteen years old. No makeup, period, buddy. So I learned how to be a little slick and a little sneaky. Overall, 90 percent of the time, I would say I was respectful and helpful and got As and Bs and wasn't fast, but like any teenagers, hey, we were teenagers. That 10 percent of the time, I did what I wanted on the unda, and it came with consequences.

You reap what you sow. It's a real true statement. But hey, it's all love, all for love, right? Wrong.

All I knew was I was going to get married and have kids and life was going to be great. I knew it would be.

My sister and I were raised and trained to be wives, not side chicks, not girlfriend #2 or #3. Period. And our parents were very clear about sex before marriage and staying virgins and respecting yourself and God.

Unfortunately, I didn't listen. I had a boyfriend that I talked to for about a year and a half, and he was pressuring me and saying I waited this long, so I lost my virginity in five minutes. It was nothing like I thought or expected, and after that first time, we broke up a month later. Shaking my head. I was young and dumb.

I so regretted not listening to my parents. Keep your treasures in a safe, young ladies. Special moments require a special king in your life, your husband. You may not understand it now, but later you will.

Love, love, love—it's gotten me in some trouble. The heart and mind and soul, be careful who you give it to the love key, connected to your emotions, to your soul. Love can send you on a roller coaster of fun and joy or wreak havoc in a real way in your life.

I had a relationship with a young man who was older than I was, and it was a really nice and cool relationship. My cousin Michelle hooked me up with Mr. Brown, but we ended up breaking up.

I got with Monie. I started talking with him. He was really sweet; we were twelve years old. The crazy part is that I got my hair done at this place called Center Stage West, and this guy John did my hair and said, "I have a nephew I want you to meet named Jamonie."

I said, "He's been my boyfriend for about two months." Weird, huh? Now he's Uncle John.

Everything in junior high was good except people trying to break us up. If it wasn't a girl who liked him or a boy who liked me, it was something else. In high school we had a brief moment when we broke up and got back together. Then when I graduated high school, that's when Monie went to prison. We broke up for about a year. I found out he had cheated on me. Yeah, long story, side eye.

So I ended up getting back with Mr. Brown for a month. He took me to Vegas for my birthday. We were in the room, I looked down, and he was asking me to marry him. I was in shock. Unfortunately, I said no. My son was two years old, and I wasn't ready to get married. We had been back together only a few weeks. I felt bad.

As soon as the plane landed back home, we broke up. It was ugly. I felt so bad, and the whole plane ride from Vegas to Oakland, he gave me the business! He was pissed, and I was so hurt that I hurt him, because I had love for him. We parted ways and didn't really speak for twenty years. It's all love.

Girls always love dads, daddy's girls. A father's love. And my dad didn't meet Mr. Brown, so imagine if I had come home married to someone my parents had never met. All hell would have broken loose.

My cousin May called me. He had gone to jail and needed me to make three-way calls for him. Boy, I tell ya. So I would for him.

One day he said, "Hey, cuz, I want you to be friends with my friend. He needs a pen pal."

I said, "I have never done that before."

"This one time. Here he goes." He gave his friend the phone.

It caught me off guard, but I wasn't rude, and I started to talk with his friend. He actually was a very nice, cool, respectable guy, so I agreed to write him and gave him my number. I'll call him King CC.

Now, I told him up front, "I'm single with a son, and his dad is in prison. I'm not looking for a relationship, and we most likely will get back together as soon as he gets out." He said OK.

After many calls and conversations and letters, I was building a friendship and was liking the man he was. He was very smart, and he loved God; he would talk about his Muslim religion, and it was very interesting. Slowly but surely, King CC was stealing my heart, and I was building love for him, which I didn't at all expect.

He was in jail for something he didn't do but got blamed for, and he was facing a whole lot of time. I believed him when he said that he was innocent, and I sent him a pic of me after a while. But he didn't send me one. He said I had to come visit him to see what he looked like. I wasn't happy, but I was curious, so I went to see him. He was handsome, and I could tell now that he saw me in person, he liked me, and I liked him too.

Your brain and heart—they sometimes don't work together, and the more time we spent talking and writing and seeing each other, the more feelings I had for him.

Monie called me. He asked me to marry him in prison.

I said, "No, you didn't ask before you went, so I'm not going to do it while you're in there."

Monie said, "We aren't together, but as soon as I get out, we are getting married."

I knew that he was getting out soon, and I didn't want any problems, so the week before Monie was released, I told King CC we couldn't be friends anymore. I was so sad.

A week later, I moved out my parents' house, and my mom threw away all the stuff I left, including all of King CC's letters. He never called back, and I didn't know any of his family info. My mom said, "I didn't know." I tried off and on to find King CC with no luck.

Long story short, for eighteen years I wondered what happened to him. It was like he had a chair in my brain or something.

One day, I got a message from his brother: King CC was getting out, and all his charges were cleared. Imagine that. I was really happy!

We spoke on the phone after twenty years, and my heart almost broke out of my chest, literally. Crazy how love is still stored in the heart.

We met in person and had lunch and talked about past and present events. We both just passed through each other's life, and we are cool friends.

The reason I nicknamed the guy that stole my heart King is because he is the only man who never disrespected me and who guarded my heart. That's why. The main thing I learned from King CC is always tell someone you love that you love them. It's all love, and I wish him the best!

When Monie got out, we got a place. A few weeks later, we went to pick out rings, and I got pregnant. It was a girl; I was happy. I had a dream her eyes were blue and her hair was gold. I said her name would be Ashley. Everything was happening so fast!

One day Monie was talking to his cousin on the phone, and I overheard the convo. He said, "Blood, she looks dead on me."

I immediately knew he was saying he had a daughter, and if that was true, our child would be daughter number three. Yes, there were actually two ladies saying they had daughters, but no DNA tests were done, and I was six months pregnant. I ran to the bathroom; he had set me up! And he had talked loud so he didn't have to tell me in person.

He said, "What's wrong with you?"

I said, "You know exactly what's wrong with me!"

I didn't feel like my daughter was going to be special to him, and he had two other daughters he had never met before. I was devastated, and I threw his ring back; then I picked it back up and went to the mall and returned it.

Now the reason we had broken up when he was in prison is that a girl said she had his baby, but he said she was lying. I didn't know what to believe.

After I had my daughter, Ashley, who was born with bright-red hair and green eyes, I was in love with her, and she looked exactly like her dad.

I ended up meeting the little girl in question. The crazy part is she was my son Lil Monie's twin! She looked like me! Her mom and I looked similar. Wow, super shocking.

Long story short, her mom didn't want a DNA test done, but she wanted a lot of money monthly, big money, or she wasn't going to come over. So she changed her number and address, and we didn't see her again. Cold games people play.

After that was over, years later, one day I was going to Reno, so we rented a car. Inside the rental car place, I turned around, and Monie had a different ring and asked me to marry him again. And I said yes!

We literally went home, packed a bag, told Auntie and Grandma what we were up to, and left for Reno, Nevada. He bought Jagged Edge and Next's album and sang to me "Girl, Let's Get Married" and "You're My Wifey." He drove me crazy, but that's love.

I was in the casino in my wedding dress, and people threw chips at us. We got almost a few thousand dollars in chips, hecka cool.

We took pictures and stayed in the casino, throwing dice, getting lucky. Then we went up to our suite and made about four calls and left messages ("We got married, y'all"). Next thing you know, we had two hundred voice mails. The family was upset; everybody was. We kept the phone off for the rest of the day. We were in trouble!

I loved the fact I was married now, and I thought it would change our relationship, but it didn't. He was doing him, and he was very much a single husband. He broke my heart many times. It was like, "Here, Nese, here's some Krazy Glue. Fix your heart." Then he would stomp on it again.

I'm a Cancer, so I guess we love hard and we are givers and loving people who are very loyal, but damn, why me? Blasting the music in the apartment, Faith Evan's song "You Used to Love Me," singing it loud, too.

My thinking was we had four kids and we had been together a long time, since we were twelve years old, so I trusted him to an extent. But when you are dealing with a liar and a cheater, it messes with the trust. I'm a very forgiving person, but I did want out of the madness sometimes. But I stayed because we had four kids, and he wasn't going to let me leave him and have the kids, so that was a problem for me.

And I thought maybe one day he would change.

Love will put you in situations, and the problem with me was I thought I could make him change, but like Monie would say, "I will never change who I am. Only if I want to. Unless I want to, you can't make me do exactly what you want." And he was right: you can't make anybody change unless the person wants to make a change.

I would pray that he would change his ways with other women and the street life, and he continued on the menu.

I didn't waste my breath, and for about three years before he was killed, we lived separate lives.

Everything that Mr. Brown said on the plane—that if I got back with Monie, he was going to dog me—came true, everything!

I sat Monie down in 2003 and told him I wasn't in love anymore; I had love for him, but I couldn't do this anymore. He could mess with anybody he wanted to; just don't ask me to have sex, because he had about three girlfriends, so that was the tip of the volcano. He would bring women to the house we lived at, around the kids, while I was at work. I found out from my five-year-old.

These are the last two straws that blew the camel's back off! I was cooking, and I heard him downstairs. He was planning a date, and I was furious. So I went and got this ring I had bought him for Father's Day, a $20,000 twenty-carat ring he had wanted. Yes, crazy, but he had pitched to me, "I'm a great father," which he was, so I got the ring.

I hid the ring. He came looking for it. "Where's my ring?"

I said, "Oh, your new girlfriend is gonna buy you a new one. You thought you was gonna go out with that ring? LOL, nope, honey. You're sure not gonna get this back."

He was upset and said, "I'm not coming back until I get this ring. I'm spending the night out."

I said, "Oh, you're telling me you gonna spend the night out? If you do, it will be dire consequences."

So he did, not one night but two, and this time I was super hot! So hot, so very hot. I spent $1,000 for every hour he was gone. Yep, $48,000 on all my bills. Let's say I cleaned out my credit and went shopping.

I went looking for him and found his car at a hotel, and I busted all his windows on his car. When I was looking through the car, I saw he had bought her perfume and watches, movie stubs, Red Lobster, so I blew up his phone. His alarm went off; he and she looked out the hotel window at me. I waved.

It was on! I'm telling you, I was outdone! Next up, my mind was racing, and I was red as a beet, boiling hot! Wanna play, huh? OK! I went back home and put sugar and fruit in the gas tank of his beloved old-school Cougar—$15,000 supercharged engine, down the drain.

I was on a roll. I gave all his clothes to homeless people. I mean, 99 percent of his clothes, to the homeless. I left him two outfits with two pairs of shoes, all mismatched, of course.

Yeah, love had me all messed up. Some people think Trinese is very sweet and nice and kind, which I am. But Nese—she will kick you in the back of the ass and keep it one thousand with you. Some people take kindness for weakness, but I'm the type to hold it all in and then go off. Sometimes overall I'm a very cool-water type of girl; I promise I am. I promise you I have never been to jail a day in my life, but that night, I almost went. The security guard wrote my license plate down, and the police came to my house and said I had broken my husband's windows.

I told the officer, "I know my rights, and I broke the windows to my car, so you can't take me to jail for breaking windows when the law states, California State community property, I own that car."

After all those *Law and Order* and *CSI* episodes, man, I was talking like a real attorney.

The officer was so mad. He said, "You're right! But your husband is gonna have to come down to clear you." So Monie went to clear my name.

It was so bad after he found out what I did that he didn't come back for three months, and I was just over it, everything!

Man, don't get me wrong. This love picture, I'm painting isn't looking pretty, but 60 percent of the time, we had a great relationship, traveled, went out, and had a lot of love, especially when it came to our kids. But the streets and other women don't belong in a marriage, and on top of that, we had other people in our business, which made it worse. When love is involved, it's a two-person deal, and once four or five people want to add their two cents, it starts getting even worse. Trust me, keep everybody out ya bizness. It's all love.

Sidenote: I was having a convo with my friend and her brother about relationships and why men cheat. That was a long convo, turned into a debate. Relationship tip from me: if you argue with your BF or hubby, and it's a little or a big fight, with all the disagreements and attitudes, do the exact same thing: grab his face and give him the biggest kiss. Kisses are 99 percent effective. But you didn't hear it from me! My little secret, 99 percent effective, didn't work one time! What worked for me may not work for you! For real.

My husband was the jealous type. He also drove me to and picked me up from work sometimes. One day I was coming out of the job, and one of my coworkers asked for some of the strawberries I had in my hand. "Aww, man!" Monie said. "Don't be asking my wife for none of her straw-berries." I was so embarrassed!

I said, "Why did you do that? He's my friend."

He said, "No, you don't have any male friends." And for eighteen years, I never talked with another man on the phone or cheated on him. Once I told him we were done, two years before he was killed, we acted like we were together for everybody else, but we were separated.

Usher says the truth hurts. I love that song, it's my truth, and I'm spill-ing my truth, some pieces of my story. I wish it weren't mine, to an extent, but it's mine, and unfortunately I messed up too. Two wrongs don't make a right. Yes, that's a fact!

Once Monie brought other women to the house while I was at work. That changed the whole game for me, and I wasn't the same anymore. He had crossed the line. What does R. Kelly say about "when a woman's fed up"? Yep, that part. He was going to have me catch a case. I had never been to jail before, ever!

He couldn't tell me nothing; I hired a divorce attorney. The attor-ney said that because he was not working, I would have to pay $2,500 a month to him. I wasn't about to do that, so I stayed but told him he would have to pay all my bills, plus some, which he did.

I never thought this would happen, but we switched shoes, and I be-came him and he became me. I became a coldhearted, numb, non caring person to his feelings. "Hey, just take care of your kids, pay the bills. I don't care what you're doing, and don't worry about me."

He gave me flowers and cards and showered me with gifts and calls and messages and lots of money, and he wanted to do this and that, just showered me with love, but I was tired of forgiving. All of it was nice, but I told him nothing would work. I was not buying it this time.

At this time Monie was like, "I can see who I want, but don't even think you can."

One day, walking into the office, I bumped into a coworker. We both weren't watching where we were going, and our stuff went flying in the air! That was the start of a friendship that went on to become more.

I will call him Mr. International. It's all a very classic tale. Yep, this is where I messed up, and my karma is my karma.

They say everyone comes into your life for a reason. That may be true, but always be careful who you let in your life.

Anyway, back to the script, Mr. International messaged me to say sorry about bumping into me, and after that message, we were cool and kept in contact here and there for a while.

I nicknamed him Mr. International because I saw he was traveling a lot and ladies loved him. I was seven years older than he was.

I gave him my number. He knew I was married with kids, but at that time we were still friends. I was separated from my husband but not divorced.

So after e-mailing, calling, and text-messaging, we decided to meet up at the new house he just bought around Christmastime. He said, "I'm gonna cook, and if I buy mistletoe, I'm gonna kiss you!"

Well, he cooked, and he bought mistletoe. Have you ever heard of falling in love on the first kiss? Right, only in the movies. I promise that happened. Shaking my head!

It wasn't even a french kiss—that's the crazy part—but that kiss sparked a whole new chain of events that I never thought I would be doing, so we decided we would wait for Valentine's Day. We went out of town, and I turned my phone off for three days. My kids were with their grandmother, and I checked in with them often but not with Monie.

We had a lot of fun, to say the least, but I knew I would have to answer for it, and while we were in LA, someone who knew Monie just so happened to film me and Mr. International together, and the person con-fronted me about it later when I got back to Oakland.

I know that person told Monie, so when I got back, it was all hell.

"Your phone was off."

I replied, "Well, you have done this to me hundreds of times. Now you know how it feels."

"Where did you go?"

"We are not together, so don't ask me nothing, just like I don't ask you nothing for years when you leave. See how it feels?"

Monie wasn't stupid; he knew something was up, but he continued to kill me with kindness, and I started feeling guilty for my actions. I even for-got our wedding anniversary. Even if we weren't together, we still would get a present for September 8, but I forgot, and he had fifteen Baby Phat presents. I cried, "I forgot like you." He had forgotten one time too.

My birthday rolled around, and Monie said, "We haven't had sex in a very long time, which tells me even if we aren't together, you are see-ing somebody, and don't get you and someone hurt." He was right, so I broke up with Mr. International.

So Mr. International and I were off and on, and I explained to him exactly how my relationship and marriage with Monie were and that I was going to get a divorce; I just didn't want to have to pay him $2,500 a month and not really see my kids.

I could tell Monie was hurt and sad, and I was too, honestly. When you want to punish someone for hurting you, you punish yourself too!

I wanted things to be cool, but after someone cheats on you repeat-edly and has two kids outside the marriage, only for you to find once he dies that he was hiding a third child as well, things just aren't the same.

The day before he was killed, he apologized for everything. We had a fun day together, and I was having second thoughts, like maybe I should just forget the past and we should start over. But I was scared. That day my sister told me two wrongs don't make a right, and she was right.

My grandmother always said never have two doors open at the same time. I never knew exactly what that meant, but I understood her statement in this situation. Being in a love triangle is not cool. I don't know how men see more than two or three women at a time, plus have wives. It's too much.

For a while Mr. International and I cooled off. I needed to take care of myself and the kids, and life was super crazy and changing pretty fast. When we did start to talk again, I was nervous about him meeting my kids after their dad's death, because everyone had two cents to say. Some people didn't want to see me with anyone for ten years plus, literally. And I had never introduced anyone to my kids before. This would be all new to them and to me.

I started off with my two girls. They were OK with meeting him. And then my younger son, and then my oldest son. Saved the best for last. I thought my kids would give him a hard time. A couple of them did, here and there, but after some time, they were pretty cool with Mr. International.

Right out of the gate, I explained to Mr. International I had four kids and didn't want any more, so I had had my tubes tied. He didn't have any kids, and he said he wasn't tripping off that, but I would ask him about it all the time. I broke up with him a few times because I had a feeling he wanted kids, and I didn't want to be selfish with that. I would break up with him, and he would be knocking on the door, saying, "We just didn't break up. What's for dinner?"

I'd say, "What's for dinner at your house?" And we would be right back together.

I'm a Cancer, born in July, so I am water, cool water, but he's a fire sign, Aries, born in April. They really don't match at all. They say opposites attract; that's a fact.

We hardly argued, but when we did, which was always about breaking up, I would defuse the argument with a kiss.

Mr. International was very sweet and kind and understanding about everything, and we went to movies, restaurants, and trips. He always wanted to, and did, help with the kids.

We got along and had lots of fun, and we both had love for each other and had no complaints in any area.

Except he was a cheater and broke my heart. That's all. I can actually laugh about it. Love makes you feel like a damn fool sometimes, but that's OK. The heart mends. It's all 143, the code number for love when texting.

One day I said a prayer and asked God, "Can I trust him? Will you, God, show me if I can?" I always say that same prayer about people in my life, and the light shines bright on different things.

Mr. International went out of town, and I was using his car. We went to get some food, my friends and my daughter and I. Nini (my daughter) left a bag on the floor where she was sitting, and under the bag, there was DNA testing paperwork.

I said, "Oh, he has a baby or a baby on the way." I was embarrassed because I was with people and they saw my reaction, upset and feeling like I couldn't trust him. Ms. Karma was there, paying me a visit, a well-deserved one.

I was hot, so I called Mr. International, but he was so nonchalant, I didn't say anything about the papers.

I parked his car at his house and started walking home, but he wanted to talk to me and meet up with me and pick me up.

I said, "You set me up! You left those papers in the car on purpose, knowing I would have your car, because you wasn't man enough to tell me."

I went home and cried, "I can't trust anybody!"

He had a son, and I was very happy for him about his having a child, because I knew deep down he wanted one.

I was going to get my tubes untied, and but I was super happy I didn't have to now. But the trust was blown, and I should have known better, just by how it all started. But we live, we learn, we love, and we make mistakes.

Making a face. Overall we had a lot of fun, and we clicked. Years went by, we both knew each other like a book, and we talked about getting married, but you can't marry a player who plays games. Not going to hap-pen while games are being played.

My main focus was God, my kids, myself, my money and bills, and hustling, thinking of ideas for how to provide for my family, period.

We got back together shortly after, but I never trusted him completely, and once I had cancer, things changed with me. A few days after my first surgery, I broke up with him because he went to the club the day after my surgery, and I thought, this isn't gonna work for me at all.

The one thing cancer did teach me is who had my back 100 percent, and that was the eye-opener that changed Nese. I got the call from King CC the day before surgery, and one thing he told me was never ever settle, never, and that stuck with me, to make that decision and take it seriously, to really not let people treat me any ole kind of way.

The crazy part about Mr. International is he's a good person, and my family has love for him, and I love his family to pieces. Hi, Momma B.

We ended up being apart for about a year, and he wanted to hook back up, so I said, "Let's meet up at Jamba Juice." But before I headed there, I said a prayer for God to show me a sign, please, if I should give him another shot.

Thirty minutes later I was in the building, and I was looking at all the pics on the wall, and lo and behold, there was one of him and another lady and kids. So I took a quick pic, sent it to him, and asked who it was, and he was having another baby with her.

I had gotten my sign, and we went our separate ways. There's a lot more to the story, but I will leave well enough alone. I miss him, but I'm happy to be single. The sizzle had fizzled out. 143 means love.

Being single for a minute was cool. I didn't have to worry about anyone but me.

On Tuesdays, I would let my daughter drive the car, and for some reason I would always leave my house key on the key ring and get locked out of the house. So one day, while waiting for her to get off work, I decided I would pick about five numbers for people I hadn't talked with in years and text them.

I picked this guy from my contacts; I will call him Handsome. He was, too!

Now I met Handsome at my BF Carisa's birthday party, and we hit it off, but he was moving fast, and I wasn't. We talked for a few months, and then we lost contact, so it had been a minute since we had spoken to each other.

I texted him: "Heyyy, how are you?"

He was like, "Who is this? And send me a pic." I sent him a pic, and he was like, "Where in the heck have you been?" He had gotten a new phone and lost my number, and I had never called back. I thought he had just stopped calling me, but my friend at work did say he was looking for me.

He said, "I wanna see you tonight." So we hooked up that night, watched movies, and were very happy to see each other.

Now Handsome is ten years older than me, he has his own business and owns his own home, and he works hard, but he's a playa.

I asked him if he was in a relationship, and he said, "No. PS. When you have to ask, you should already know." He said, "I'm dating people, but no relationship." I told him I was single.

From that one text, we started texting and calling each other and spending time with each other, and I really started to like him. After about four or five months, I was like, I know I'm not catching feelings for him, but I was.

After about a year and a half, I asked him again if he was seeing anybody, and he was like, no, but he was going on dates.

Well, one day I was with a friend, and she said, "I'm gonna hook you up with somebody."

I said, "I'm talking with someone." I said Handsome's name, and she spit her food out across the room.

She said, "No you're not talking to him. He has been in a relationship with my friend for over six years." Now, to hear that hurt, because I don't like to have trust issues with people, but at the end of the day, we were not together or married.

So I confronted him, and he told me he was in two relationships, but he was unhappy in both and was happy with me. He wanted to know who snitched on him. I wasn't going to give up my trusted contact, but I did end things with the quickness with Handsome.

I ended up having love for him, and I felt the love, but the lies? No, thank you. I don't care how handsome you are.

One thing he did teach me is older men play games just like younger men do. That's too bad. I let him know, why would I want two other women's man? Why would I want to be number three? Are you crazy? Must be!

I put his number on block for a few months, but then I took it off, because the one thing that made me think I could be his friend was that he was asking his friends about hospitals for cancer patients and how he could help me with beating cancer. Now that is love, so because of that, he has a special spot in my heart.

But I told him, "Hey, do what you like, but you are going to end up old and alone with nobody if you keep playing around." To each his own. I wish Handsome the best and all the Twixes and Kit Kats in the world.

Not that I'm really into signs, but they say Cancers and Scorpios are a love match, and I have to admit my match is with a cool water sign.

My friend Janet said, "Momma bear, just open an online dating site." So like a dummy, I did. "Try something new and stop being a homebody," she said.

So I went on a date with a very nice guy. I will call him J. J took me to play pool, and I whooped his butt two times in a row, and he was a very sore loser. He started to text, and we would talk on the phone. After a few weeks, we got really cool.

When I got back from Maui, we went on a second date to the Cheesecake Factory; I love cheesecake. While at dinner he started singing. I had never had a man serenade me in public. That was so cute! It was cute and romantic. Things were going way too good, which had me thinking.

And one day I saw him at the light across from me, and he was with his family and kids. It looked like he was with his baby momma, whom he said he wasn't with anymore, but it was smelling fishy to me.

He called me an hour later. I didn't answer. Then the next day, he said, "I called you."

I said, "I saw you with someone else."

After that I didn't call, and he didn't call. I just didn't have time for lies again.

I'm not rushing love. I know when God sends me someone, I will be ready for that day.

I got a message on Facebook from someone I had gone to summer school with. He sent a few messages, and we started to text. Then we had a few calls and decided to meet up.

Well, we met up, and let's just say it was thirty minutes of craziness.

I parked the car and saw him pulling up. He looked a little tipsy. He kept backing up and reparking. Shaking my head. But I don't judge. I was like, maybe I'm tripping.

He got out and gave me a hug, and then he started to smoke. I don't smoke—strike 1. Then he started saying how he was my deceased husband's friend—strike 2. Oh, heck no.

Then he said, "So what are we?"

I said, "We are two people saying hello," but I was thinking of ways to say good-bye.

He was talking about wanting a relationship, and I said, "Wait, wait. This is just a quick hello and how are you, a fifteen- to twenty-minute meet and greet, nothing more."

Strike 3 was when he said, "Follow me to my house."

I said, "No. No, thank you."

I started to get out of his car to return to my car, but he got upset and followed me to my car. He said, "What's gonna happen when I don't give a f*** anymore?"

I said, "I guess you won't be caring, but I'm about to leave. You have a good night."

He got in his car and rear-ended two cars on his way out. Next thing I know, he's between two women yelling. I was like, wow, this is why I stay home.

He called me, ten minutes later and said, "Man, I want a do-over."

I said, "Things happen."

With the quickness, I placed his number on the block list and was so happy to be single. I don't need extra problems. All I could do was laugh, and I haven't been on a date since.

Your heart and your brain go through so much because of love, but they keep going. In life, love will teach you a lot of lessons.

I think the best kind of love is for your kids. A mother's love.

Saying a prayer and God answering it—now that's love.

Love for family and friends and the little things, doing something kind for someone—now that's love.

If more people gave out more love, the world would be so much more filled with love. Sounds lovely.

I can honestly say I love to do nice things for others. It fills me with love, and I feel good. It makes me happy to see other people happy. I love it!

I want to show people love, even when they don't deserve it. That's the part in your heart when you have unconditional love and when you use it. It shocks people sometimes, and sometimes people couldn't care less, but at the end of the day, kill them with kindness. It's what Grandma would say and do. "Just kill them with kindness, girl."

Love has taught me a lot, and I can say I have grown up more to really be grateful for all the life lessons love has taught me. With the good and bad, I will be more prepared and less afraid to let my guard down with someone new.

Like they say, one monkey does not stop the show. Yep, I'm sure someone can relate.

I read this once: believe you deserve it, and the universe will serve it.

If you always believe you will get someone not so cool, you will; he's available.

Claim love, smile, dress up like the queen you are, and attract the king looking and waiting for you. Love awaits, for you and me.

It's November 14, 2016. I'm currently about to do chemo #4 in a few days. I have decided that I'm going to really focus on beating cancer this fourth time, and I'm going to put me first and love me, love Nese, love Trinese.

When spreading love all around, remember to love you. After all I wrote about love, I know that I have experience and will make better choices. Love has taught me I'm not perfect, and nobody is; we all make mistakes.

I can honestly say I'm not looking back at all the bad things anymore but looking forward to only great things for my future. I'm claiming it.

Love is a beautiful thing to have; cherish it! And never take it for granted!

Much love, XOXOXO,

Nese

CHAPTER 16

— ❧ —

Ms. Hustla $$$$

If you don't work, you don't eat. Never saw a lazy hustle
get you anywhere. Get up and make things happen.

—NESE

"On My Hustle," by the Mekanix

THAT'S ME, A hustler. I'm the little girl who had the lemonade stand, and I'm the little girl who gave all the cookies and Popsicles at my house away to the neighborhood kids. All my friends, yep.

That's my downfall to the hustle: I'm too nice.

I had a job in junior high school selling newspapers. Then I was a waitress in high school. After school I went to work at my aunt Anetha's soul food restaurant and made fat tips from NFL and baseball players who ate there.

I have sold makeup, bulletproof vests, uniforms, and cell phones. I worked at a few telephone companies and sold home products. Lots of sales jobs. I sold purses, earrings, scarves, clothes, and peach cobbler... lots of peach cobbler.

Whether going to the casino or selling things at the flea market or online, I'm always thinking of ways to make money. And yes, I tell my kids, "You better find a hustle, a little business." They have sold candy and had lemonade stands too and washed cars, sold cupcakes, and sold snacks at lunch to classmates, little hustlers.

My favorite hustle is the stock market. You really have to know the game to be successful. So I started studying rich billionaires and millionaires to see what they invest in and going to different websites to see what stock was number one in the world and what stock was ordered the most worldwide.

That paid off, and for a few months, I had a really lucky streak. Let's just say in a week I made what I made in nine months working at a desk, and that was exciting! The stock that was the most successful was a chemotherapy stock, imagine that. Yep, and just like that, the market changes. You really gotta know what you're doing, or you can lose, big too.

When I got diagnosed with cancer for the fourth time, I got really depressed, and my winning streak crashed. I wasn't thinking positive for a few weeks, and I wasn't making money either. I was losing, and I stopped with stocks and hustling. After a month I slowly started back up with stocks and with writing, and I feel like I'm back in the game.

I have been off of work for a year. I left my desk job of twelve years, and I'm happy that I took the jump, and I'm doing different hustles. I'm not as stressed as I was, but I miss seeing all my coworker family a lot. But I'm very happy I'm becoming a writer, an author, Ms. Hustla chasing her dreams. Guess I get it from my grandparents and parents. They all had hustles. Get out and hustle, baby. Make money.

Next up I'm currently taking classes for my real estate license to see what that's all about.

Hang around people who are more successful, and you exchange ideas, combine great minds.

I was listening to some of my sista's friends. Ms. Kenya really pushed me to jump to the next level and not be afraid to make changes and be on your hustle to get that money.

The main thing is believing God will take care of you and guide you the right direction. Having faith is important. God will always provide and bless you. Blessings.

The only thing is we have to put forth effort to be successful and use God's gifts he gave us, and I believe we all have a purpose.

The best part of being Ms. Hustla is I love to help my family and friends and be able to go out and have fun. I'm not at the level I want to be at, but I'm working on it and getting ready for my next level, and I'm bringing somebody with me. I'm teaching my children to be debt-free, with excellent credit and businesses, and to be able to help others. That would be great.

And I'm not going to let my having cancer be an excuse. I'm on my hustle, sick or not sick. At the same time, I'm staying on top of my health, because your health is your wealth. I'm taking extra good care of my health, exercising and eating right, taking vitamins and herbs, getting massages, eating organic, relaxing, drinking lots of water, and staying in prayer. Man, take care of yourself: having fun, listening to music, and watching funny movies. Staying in a positive mood and being happy. It helps the hustle. It just seems everything goes better when the energy is great!

Get around some great people that want to see you succeed, and get a mentor. I have a few of them.

Don't limit yourself. No limits. 2017 is coming up in three weeks. I'm working on my game plan. What about you? Hey, let's get it!

See it and believe it, and it's going to happen! I'm on my hustle. See you at the top.

SURROUND YOURSELF AROUND BUSINESS MINDED PEOPLE, SUCCESS CAN BE CONTAGIOUS.

CHAPTER 17

Best Friend, That's My Best Friend

Friends...how many of us have them?

—WHODINI

My sister Tiffany and me

I TALKED EARLIER about my best friends in junior high, V and Ashonti. Now I will talk about my other BFFs.

I'm really blessed to say I have had at least eight to ten amazing friends, and the list can go on, besides my sister Tiffany being my number one, my ace. My sister and I—we have each other's back, and we always are there for each other, always!

I remember when my sister got her leg amputated (because of cancer), if anybody made fun of her, they had to deal with me, and I would be right behind her, looking at them crazy. Please don't mess with my sis! Ha-ha, please.

I used to work at a store, and I met a lady who did security there, and we became very close. Her name was Nicole, a.k.a. Shugga. We would go to places to shop. We loved Starbucks and caramel fraps, going out to eat, and talking on the phone. Once she told me her mom was murdered and I told her my grandmother was, we connected.

One day at work, she got a phone call that her dad had just been murdered. I was the first to give her a hug, and she left work to go to the scene.

We both left the store we worked at in 2004, Actually, I was fired. My boss wanted to hire his niece, and I overheard that convo, and that day they let me go. But I made them pay me for it. The manager fired at least ten staff and replaced them with his own relatives, and I was the last on his list. Discrimination.

But in return it was a big blessing! I ended up getting a better job with three times the pay and better benefits, so I'm not complaining. It was because of Nicole that I found the job. She was the security at the new location. It took me about six months to get hired at my new job at the telephone company. By then Nicole was at a new location. But we spoke at least five days a week for at least fourteen years. Nicole was my second sister, and she always gave great advice and told it like it was. We never had one argument, not one.

One day we were eating and talking about my new job. She said, "How do you like it?"

I said, "It's cool."

She said, "I used to talk to this young guy there." She never said his name. To think that was the guy I was talking to at that moment, as I later found out. (Another chapter, trust me.)

Nicole loved my peach cobbler and vanilla ice cream and my chicken salad! The year before I got cancer, all of a sudden, she became totally blind. It was crazy! Man, I could not believe it! Shugga loved her two sons, my adopted nephews, loved them to pieces. Anthony and Kwame, love you both!

One night, on August 11, 2014, Nicole called me. I told her I had to call her back because I had company. Well, the company stayed late, and I didn't call her back, thinking I would call her in the morning. I went to work and saw four missed calls from her, so on my break, I called back, and her brother said, "Nicole died this morning, Trinese, and we are waiting for the morgue to pick her up."

I was so shocked. I couldn't believe it! She was forty years old. Gone too soon! Gone too soon! I so miss her! RIP, Nicole. Man, I couldn't believe it! This really hurt. My friendship with Nicole will be forever missed!

Working at my job for almost twelve years, I made quite a few close relationships.

I will start with Carisa. We sat next to each other for nine years, and I would say at least six of those years, we were very, very close. Carisa was the sweetest and kindest person I have ever met, ever! She was a few years older than me, a mom, married, and a homeowner. She was really good at her job; everybody loved Carisa!

We would often hang out, go shopping, take each other out for our birthdays, and talk a lot on the phone. After work she would give me rides home, if I didn't walk. I lived off the lake, and it was a fifteen-minute walk to work, so that was the cool part.

When I first got breast cancer, Carisa left me a message on my voice mail, crying. I was so touched. She came by the house and cleaned up, did grocery shopping, and called and texted every day when I was going through chemo. I had to make her go home. I was so thankful for Carisa!

She also wanted to play matchmaker. At her birthday party, I met someone, and we hit it off a few times (off and on—I talk about that in the love/relationship chapter).

One day after work, we both stood up, looked at each other, and were so glad to be going home, tired. We had had a long day. Those customers will show no mercy. Anyway, she took me home, and my legs were feeling kind of funny, like I couldn't feel them. The next day I couldn't walk. I had severe neuropathy. I went to the hospital. Next thing you know, I was admitted. I had side effects from chemo, and I had to learn how to walk again.

Carisa texted me that she was sorry to hear I was in the hospital. I told her I would call her in the morning. Well, in the afternoon, her son called me and said she had just died. Her son then came to the hospital to visit me. There it was; his mom had just passed, April 17, 2014. Wow, she was forty-something!

Rewind six months, I had just told Nicole and Carisa the doctors said I had only a few years maybe, and they both said, by coincidence, on separate phone calls, "We are gonna be like the Golden Girls."

Now both of them were gone before me. That's when it really hit me: nothing is promised, nothing. I'm still close to both my BFFs' children. I'm going to make sure I keep in touch with them and show them love! RIP, BFFs Nicole and Carisa.

Prayers go out to both families, Big Joe and the kids. Love you, fam!

Carisa and me

Grandma Margie taught me how to make peach cobbler, and everybody loved it! That's why Naima, a.k.a. Ny-Ny, nicknamed me Peaches. Ny-Ny is a boss. She's a very smart and talented young mom whom I can see moving up in the company.

When I first got breast cancer, not too long after, her mom also went through it as well. Do you know she was helping us both through our treatments? She would come over and clean up after work, and she always checked on me. Ny-Ny is the type of friend you need when the chips are down. I will never forget all the effort she put into our friendship. She was an angel to help me fight cancer all four times! Love my Ny-Ny!

OK, so Monique, a.k.a. Momma Mo-Mo, is the friend everyone should have! I don't know what I would have done without her for the last twelve-plus years. Two words: awesome and amazing! My angel/sista/friend. One thing I know: out of all the people I know, Mo-Mo lives life to the fullest. Whenever I'm down, she has a comedy show ticket, or we go to the spa or out to dinner. Momma Mo-Mo definitely helps me fight cancer each and every time!

Monique, a.k.a. Momma Mo-Mo (she thinks she's my momma), and me

My cousin Berta Jean is my motivation to be a boss. Don't talk, do. Keep it moving; keep it pushing; don't stop moving, being a queen and diva with it. I have to say, watching her helped me put the pedal to the metal with my book at Olympic speed. My cousin is always someone who supports me, and I support her as well. She's a queen, and when you hang around people who want to go higher, they lift you up, and she's lifting you and doing it in heels too!

Queen Nese and Queen Berta—love you!

Berta's book, *A Boss Diva's Daily Devotional*—available at Amazon and all retail stores. Go, cuzn!

OK, my sis Janet—all I can say about her is she is an earth angel, my earth angel! Always, always has my back, great advice, smart and loving, my sister from anotha motha. Love you, Janet.

My Tess! Hey, Tessa. Now Tessa is my gurl, and if I needed to have anybody told off in a nice spicy way, I would tell Tess. At the same time, she's the sweetest friend you can have! XOXOXO, my Tess.

Tessa, Janet, and me on my last day at work—miss you!

My friend Eureka, a.k.a. Peach Cobbla Lova, always shows support and love and always asks when the book is going to be done. I'm on it! Thank you, Eureka, for the push and inspiration to keep pushing! Hi, Eureka!

People always ask me, "How do you do it?" God and my angel friends—that's how.

During chemo, Momma Mo-Mo, Ny-Ny, and my friend Toni Lynn would come and take turns cleaning up. I was really thankful for that and appreciated the help. Thank you, my sistas.

This picture is of Toni Lynn and Monique and me getting massages and lunch!

My best friends forever are my baby girls. Mommy loves you.

Since cancer scared the heck out of me, for a minute I started to meet up with old friends and get out more. Here's Kimmy and my cousin Tantosha and me having lunch and reconnecting. We had a great time! Love you guys!

Here's a selfie with my friend Frenchelle on my last day at work. We sat next to each other at work, and she's a real sweetie. Miss ya, gurl. XOXO

Me, my BF Ashonti, my good friend Tiniece,
and Ashonti's best friend Lashonda

CHAPTER 18

When Cancer Knocks

Who is it? It's me, cancer.

I HAVE ALWAYS loved the color pink, always. To me it's a very pretty color, and it's bright. I have loved it all my life. I love to wear pink lipstick. The MAC color Nicki Minaj is my favorite. I have a lot of things pink.

I have experienced the deaths of close relatives. My grandparents all passed away. My grandmother and both my grandfathers died of different types of cancer. I would always see different things in the store that would donate money to breast cancer, and sometimes I would buy them. You see the commercials about the walks and the pink ribbons and stuff, and you go about your way. Until one day, it hits close to home!

Two and a half years ago, my sister and I planned a trip. We were going to go to Mardi Gras to visit our family in the NOLA, a.k.a. New Orleans. We hadn't been to see our family in many, many years, so we thought, OK, in five months we would head out there.

About a week later, my sister said, "Hey, I was taking a shower, and I found a lump. I'm going to go get it checked out." She went to the doctor, and then said she had to go back in a week to get it checked out with a mammogram. Then we talked on the phone, and she said they were going to do a lumpectomy and she needed to do a biopsy.

So my sister did the biopsy and said she would get results back in a week or two. I was a little worried, but she said it was a small lump, and the doctor made it seem like it would be an in-and-out thing, so no worries!

I don't remember the exact date. All I remember was I was on my way home after work, and I was parking the car outside my apartment when my phone rang. It was my sister Tiffany. She said, "I have my biopsy test back, and it came back that I have breast cancer in my left breast, and instead of a lumpectomy, I will need to have my left breast removed."

It took all of twenty seconds for the lump in my throat to burst, and I just started to boohoo, cry and cry and cry.

Tiffany said, "Man, you didn't even give me a chance to cry yet." I pulled myself together and said I was sorry. We canceled the trip that we had planned, and I was just sick to my stomach, scared.

I was the older sister, and my baby sister had cancer. She was thirty-four years old, and I was thirty-six. She was a single mother of two kids. Why my sister? Like, why her? My world had crashed! I didn't want to believe this. I hate you cancer, breast cancer.

We talked for a few minutes; then she had to go so she could tell other family members. My sister is my best friend, and the thought of losing her was beyond belief. I stayed in my car in front of my apartment crying for twenty minutes. I went from shock to lump in throat, crying, mad, then OK. I had to be there for my sister and do what I could for her.

Tiffany was diagnosed with bone cancer at the age of nine. One day when we were kids, we were cleaning up our room. It was really messy, and my dad said, "Clean up this room." We were slow, so he came in and messed up the room more and said, "Now clean all of it up! And you have two hours to have this room spotless." I mean, it was so messed up.

All of a sudden, Tiffany said, "My knees hurt," and sat down.

I told her, "Hey, I'm not cleaning all this by myself." I thought she was playing. But her knee looked a little swollen, so I cleaned up the room, and my mom made a doctor's appointment for the next day. The doctor said she probably had water in her knee and she would be OK, no x-rays or anything.

It turned out it was bone cancer, and after a few weeks, it became very large. My mom found a place in Mexico that would help her naturally instead of with chemotherapy, because the doctors wanted to amputate her leg and start chemotherapy. My sister did the treatment out of the States, but the hospital in the United States and other family members joined forces, the courts made a decision on her medical behalf, and she was forced to have her leg amputated.

I always wanted to protect her. She was very strong. She did chemo for almost seven years, so to hear that she had cancer and had to do chemo again was heartbreaking.

Tiffany was in and out of the hospitals. Two weeks out of the month, she would stay there, so I spent many nights sleeping at the hospital, she was only nine at the time.

My sister had her surgery, and it was an in-and-out procedure. My aunt stayed with her for a month, and then she started chemo. I would come every two weeks and spend every other weekend.

Then my car broke down.

Then my son was getting off the bus, and an old classmate from two years prior shot him twice, with the bullets ricocheting through his heart, stomach, lung, and chest. There it was: my son was on life support, I had no car, and My sister had just had her second chemo treatment and was very sick but was at the side of my son's bed.

The doctor said he had a 50/50 chance, and I started sobbing. Tiffany handed me tissue, and I was just like, wow! Life was beating us up right now. I told my sister to go home and get some rest. For six months I took off work for my son, and one or two weekends a month, I would go out there to check on my sis.

Prayers, Prayers, and More Prayers

If it were not for the praying, I would have given up. God always answers my prayers, and I'm very thankful for that. My sister had always had a positive attitude. Always! I have never seen or heard her be negative or complain about her situations, ever. She keeps on going, doing way more than people with two legs. She's the spunky, take-no-mess-attitude, will-not-be-mistreated, tell-you-how-it-is, keep-it-real, more aggressive spirit. I'm the strong and sweet, quieter, nicer sister, so to speak, when it comes to getting hurt or someone taking my kindness for weakness. My sister would always say, "You're too nice." She never liked to see me get hurt, and that's something that I learned about the hard way in life—being too nice to the wrong people.

My sister did chemo for a year, six months of doing three chemo treatments and six months of doing one. I watched as she lost her hair, eyebrows, and eyelashes and chemo made her gain about fifteen to twenty pounds. I saw her being tired and sick and then getting better each month toward the end of the year.

In June, we planned to go to LA in July to go shopping for school clothes and then drive to Las Vegas and celebrate my sister's last chemo treatments.

It was July 19, 2012, my birthday.

I had planned to work just four hours, leave early, go to the nail salon and hair shop, buy an outfit, and go out to dinner. I normally went to Reno every year; for ten years straight I did that. Then I said I would change it up and start doing Vegas. If I didn't do Vegas, I would do a "do me" weekend with Victoria's Secret and See's Candies, get myself a purse, earrings, perfume, nails, hair, and eyebrows, and just have a fun weekend treating myself. I make sure I do this four weekends out of the year, a make-time-for-yourself holiday.

But before I could even get off work, one of my kids got into some trouble and was in juvenile hall on my birthday. Man, my day was not going so well.

I got off at one o'clock and found all the info I needed about what happened, and I was feeling down. So my little sisters Faith and Chanel came over and took me out to P.F. Chang's for dinner. They told me to get dressed, so I took a shower, but I realized I hadn't done anything for myself. So I said to myself, "Well, at least I have my health."

I was sitting on the bed in my towel, and I said a prayer, thanking God for everything I had and counting all my blessings, but mainly in my prayer, I thanked God for my health. I said amen. Then something, which I know was nothing but God, told me to lie down and do a breast self-exam, so I did.

Fresh out of the shower, the perfect time, I lay down and raised my left arm and started checking the breast in a circular motion. I didn't find anything. But at the end I found it to be very hard at the side of my left breast, so I checked the right. It felt fine. I checked the left again, and it was the size of a dollar coin, bigger than a quarter. I checked the right again to compare.

I called my sister. She told me I better get that checked ASAP. I said "OK. But I started my period today, out of all days, and when I'm on my period, my breasts are tender. So I will in a few weeks if it's still there."

Mind you, when my sister said a year and a half before that she had a lump, I made an appointment and got a mammogram. I was just fine, so I was like, what could have happened in a year and a half?

My sister came by my house, and a week later, after my birthday, she asked if I had gone to the doctor.

I told her, "No. I'm waiting for my next period, and if I have the hard spot on the side in three weeks, I will go."

I waited another week, and I said, "If this is still hard and lumpy, I will not wait until my next period." It was! So I made an appointment with the ob-gyn. The nurse did the exam and confirmed that it was a lump. She took a Sharpie and made marks on the exact spot for the x-ray tech. The next day I did a mammogram and also x-rays.

During the mammogram, the tech said she wanted to take a second test to make sure. I saw it light up red on the side of the lump, and I saw red lines on my veins. I'm no tech, but I didn't like what I saw. Then she said I needed to do a third test for the doctors. Then I did x-rays.

The doctor came in and said, "This looks like the beginning stages," but he did not say "cancer."

Talk about scared to death.

It was Friday, and I made an appointment on Monday for a biopsy.

I left the doctor's office, sat outside the door, called my sister, and told her, "They think it's the beginning stages." But I didn't use the word "cancer."

She said, "You have got to be f***ing kidding me."

I said no, and I started to bawl, crying in the lobby in front of the breast cancer center in front of fifty people just looking.

My ride came to pick me up, my boyfriend at the time. He said, "It's going to be OK. Just think positive."

I told him what they said.

He said, "Don't claim it."

I said, "You're right." But my body in that area, my left breast, was hot. It felt like a small luau party inside of me. I was stressed out, scared. I went straight to my room and couldn't wait until the next week to get this biopsy done.

I went in, and the nurse practitioner said I was supposed to get six to eight shots in the area. When I tell you that was the most painful biopsy ever, it was like putting a small needle inside of a rock-solid marble, and that's exactly what it was. I cried so badly she did only four biopsy tests. She saw how painful it was for me.

The nurse practitioner said it would take a week for the results, so I was anxious for them, very anxious.

I told my aunt, sister, brother, parents, boyfriend, and very best friend, but I did not tell my kids.

That was very, very hard, and with my kids' father, my husband, being murdered in 2005, that made it even harder. I didn't want them to worry; I didn't want to see them cry. I didn't want them to think, what if Mom dies? We will be orphans. I really didn't want that.

August 27, 2012

I was at work, on my break. I got a call. The nurse practitioner said, "Hello, I have your results, and it came back positive: you have breast cancer. But it's not the end of the world. You just have a small lump, and you'll have a lumpectomy, and it will be over."

I told two of my managers, "I want to go home." My manager gave me a ride home, and I was in shock, dire shock. This couldn't be real. I called my mom, dad, sister, brother, best friend, and boyfriend and decided that within the next week, I would tell my kids.

I made an appointment with the surgeon, and she told me that the lump was in the early stages, stage 2 or 3, and I caught it very early. But because the cancer had traveled to my left nipple, she wanted to remove the left breast.

I burst into tears. What happened to what the nurse practitioner said just a few days ago, a lumpectomy? I was very upset! I was like, why did she tell me the wrong info?

My aunt was there for support, and she sidetracked me with, "You want me to remove my left breast, I will."

I said, "No, Auntie." In the midst of tears, she made me laugh.

I met with so many nurses and doctors. I did genetic testing with my sister; BRC1 AND BRC2 genes were both negative. FYI: A lot of women don't know you can be born with those genes and will be more likely to have or get breast cancer. So get tested!

I called so many family members on my mom's and dad's side to see if anyone had breast cancer; no one did. Only diabetes was a major family illness.

I met my oncologist. He said, "OK, you have to do twenty-eight treatments of chemo every three weeks." Six months of four chemo treatments, six months of two chemo treatments. Then he made a chart.

"This is how we know if you're a survivor. You make it past three years, five years, seven years, and ten years. If you are alive past five years, then ten years, then we know you're a survivor, but we don't really know until then."

The doctor was smiling. I was pretty pissed that he was in a happy mood, telling me. He smelled like he had had a cocktail. I'm serious, too!

Because my sister had breast cancer, it made me a higher risk. So I decided to do the left breast.

What did my sister and I do in the last two years to get breast cancer? I began to think back to all the wrongs I had done to get this disease. I began searching and searching the Internet. That's scary, so many stories.

One thing I knew: I put on thirty extra pounds. I wasn't eating healthy all the time; half the time I was. I was stressed out. I put my cell phone in my bra on the left side and put the headphones on while washing dishes—wrong move. I didn't exercise a lot, maybe twice a week.

I told my girls I had breast cancer. My younger girl was pretty strong. She didn't cry in front of me, but my older daughter cried and cried and cried. She was very sad and said, "No, Mommy, no." I felt the same. That was a very sad day.

I got an appointment for surgery September 27. My life was rapidly changing fast. I went out on disability, and on the night before my surgery, my eldest daughter cried all night like a newborn baby.

September 27

Surgery was at nine o'clock in the morning.

I was up at six o'clock in the morning, getting ready, scared, literally scared.

At seven o'clock, my sister-in-law and mother-in-law came to take me to the hospital.

I took a shower and got dressed and did my hair. I had my friend take some pictures of me holding my breasts. They didn't come out so well. So I called my daughter to see if she could get some better ones. It was so funny; I was standing and taking pictures, and my daughter asked, "Mom?" LOL, girl, just take the pics. They came out cool.

Two days before my surgery, my friend Monique "Mo" took me out to Kincaid's, and I had steak and shrimp. I was glad I got out. I got a lot of support from my job; my coworkers are the best!

I got a lot of calls, messages, and support that I really needed from my parents, siblings, friends, and family.

It was eight thirty. The plastic surgeon was drawing on my upper body with a black marker. They put me in this really big blue body suit.

Before my surgery, I had about twelve people there for support. Right before my surgery, I began to cry. My brother said, "Why are you crying? Are you OK?"

I said, "No!"

As I reached the surgery area, that was when it hit home: You are really about to do this, Trinese. Both of your breasts. Since my sister had

105

cancer in one breast and I had it one breast, doctors felt it would be safer for me to do both since it's a higher risk factor.

On the surgery table, there were bright lights. Lots and lots of tools and equipment. There was my doctor. My plastic surgeon wiped my tears away and said, "Why are you crying? Everything is going to be OK." They were all smiling.

That's all I remember.

I went into a deep sleep. For the next nine hours, I had surgery. When I came to, I asked my doctor if I had to do chemo, and she said, "Yes, you have breast cancer and HER2." What is HER2? It keeps producing cancer cells even if the breast tissue is removed. So for extra precaution, chemo is done for a year.

When I woke up, there were lots of family and friend visits. I was really drugged up and in so much pain.

I also discovered I didn't have breast implants in; I had breast expanders. These are plastic things in your chest to make sure you stretch your skin for the implants. Because I was doing four chemo treatments for six months and then two for six months, I couldn't get implants for six months, because the chemo was too hard-core.

It was six months of pure hell from the expanders and the chemotherapy. The first day at the hospital, I cried; I wasn't happy at all. I had a "why me?" phase that didn't go away for a few months. No, maybe all year!

Two weeks after surgery, I cut my hair really short to get ready for chemo. Then, after the first dose, I let my daughters shave my head. They had fun!

The first dose of chemo involved sitting for eight hours and getting four chemo treatments, and it was pain from the second it hit the IV. By the time I got to eight hours, I wanted to just die. I wanted to scream, cry, and yell. I could feel my blood cells pop, or should I say die.

Your muscles and your bones are in dire pain. You're very weak, your stomach is on fire, and you have diarrhea hundreds of times a day. You can barely walk, you have hot flashes, and you lose all hair everywhere—eyelashes, eyebrows, nose hairs. When I say no hair any-where, I mean none. And you have no color, meaning I was gray some days and white the next—so not cool.

The first few months, I did a lot of crying and being sad and not used to doing anything. I missed not being busy. My aunt Eldora really helped me. So did my two girls, parents, siblings, mother-in-law, aunts, and uncles.

Discharge from the hospital was horrible. I couldn't get my nurse to give me pain meds. The nurse said, "You're not going to have these meds at home."

I began to pray and cry, and another nurse came in with meds and gave me some before I left. She was the best. I told the nurse who didn't give me meds, "Try getting both your breasts removed and on day two you don't get pain meds." I stormed out of the hospital upset!

My doctor said I would be in the hospital for five days but dis-charged me on day 3, and I had to scramble to find a ride because I told everyone five days, so all my help made plans thinking I would be in the hospital.

My aunt Eldora helped for about three months, and my two daugh-ters also helped out, which I really appreciated.

After about six months of the hard-core chemo, I had another surgery and got the expanders removed and the breast implants put in. I went from a DD to a size C, so I was a different size, but I got a breast uplift as well, and I was very happy with my plastic surgeon and the work he had done. Three weeks later I was not in as much pain from surgery and healed fast.

I did another six months of chemo, and after the treatments, I did a CT scan, which showed I no longer had cancer. YES!

I was beyond happy! So glad it was over, and a few weeks later, I went back to work. Glad one year of chemo was done and I was back to a normal life.

Thank God! Celebrating the new year with my fam!

Me after my daughters shaved my head in 2013. My first time having a bald head, nickname Amber Nese.

CHAPTER 19

∽

Hi, It's Me,
Cancer, Again

THIS IS ME celebrating my birthday, and yes, I'm in San Francisco getting my issue of garlic noodles and garlic crab and appletini. My hair is just starting to grow back, and I'm happy. It's my fortieth; I made it! But wait, not so quick. Hi, it's me, cancer, again.

After going through chemo for a full year and through about three surgeries, a double mastectomy, I was ready to get my life back on track.

I was very independent during my year with breast cancer. I had help from my mom, dad, sisters, brother, aunts, uncles, cousins, mother-in-law, father-in-law, kids, friends, and coworkers. They showed me love and teamwork. It was a rough year, and I was so glad it was over.

It was good to be back at work after a year on disability and staying at home. I wanted to get out of the house and was super happy I wasn't sick every day.

When you have breast cancer, one day you look like yourself; the next month you look like a cancer patient, like, who is this person? I didn't know who I was when I looked in the mirror, and I had to rebuild my confidence because it became low, sad to say.

Back at work, everyone was so nice and loving. I really missed them, and after a few months of training, it was back to business as usual, back to the calls and customers, sales and expectations.

Every three months, I would go to visit my oncology doctor, and she would say I was fine and had no cancer, so I was very happy about that.

But one day I had a feeling something wasn't right. When I shaved under my left arm, it felt like a golf ball was under my arm. So I made a doctor's appointment, and I asked the doctor to please do a biopsy. I waited about a week for results, and I got a call that I had cancer again in my lymph nodes. But I had just had a scan a few months ago, no cancer, so I was confused.

After being back at work for about nine months, I had to leave again and go back out on disability. I was over it! I had to tell my family and kids that cancer was back for the second time.

I was scared and worried, and I hated that I was once again going to be sick and have to rely on others again. And going back and forth on disability money was not cool.

One thing that saved me was my 401(k). Unfortunately I had to use my 401(k), and I used it so many times I can't count, to help me with emergency after emergency. So I called and got $9,000 out my 401(k), and then I called and started my disability paperwork, and it was a relief that I didn't have to worry somewhat about bills. I began to call all my utilities and pay them up for at least six months, and I started planning and budgeting my finances.

After telling my family what was going on, stage 3 breast cancer reoccurrence, I began chemo for six months, and after chemo the doctors said surgery. I knocked out the six months of chemo and got another CT scan, and the scan showed no cancer. The doctors stated I didn't have to remove my lymph nodes if I didn't want to, but I decided to go ahead and remove a few lymph nodes.

So glad I did. My first two lymph nodes had cancer that didn't show up on the CT scan. Imagine that.

After surgery, I was told I was cancer-free; it was completely gone.

Healing up took about a month or two. After about eight months, I recovered from chemo and surgery, and after about nine months, I went back to work. Yes, cancer-free!

But my mind was kind of iffy with trusting what the doctors were saying, so I kept asking, "Are you sure?" I went back and forth to different appointments, and my doctor said, "Stop worrying. Stop doctoring yourself. You are fine." I was like, OK, but a piece of me wasn't sure.

Back at work my job was closing its location, and we had three weeks to relocate. I hadn't been back a month. I couldn't just up and move to another state, and I couldn't start a long commute to a new location just coming off chemo.

So I left my job of almost twelve years; I felt like my back was up against the wall. They gave me my 401(k), my pension, and $50,000 and six months' benefits. Sounds real good, but that's not a whole lot of money to last a long time.

I was worried. But I knew it was time, my time. The doctors kept saying, "This job is gonna kill you. You are gonna keep getting cancer and die." That was what about five doctors told me, so I listened.

Because I was going to leave my job within a month, I called my doctor and said, "Hey, I know you said no cancer, but run another CT scan.

I'm about to lose my job, and I wanna make sure before I lose my medical benefits."

A few weeks later, she ordered another scan. I took the test and went to Vegas for two weeks. She said the results might take about ten days.

I had fun visiting family, my niece Angel and nephews Paris and Raul, and sis Olfe. We always have a ball.

I got an e-mail that the doctor wanted me to come in. I e-mailed her back and said, "Call me." I just knew it was bad.

She said, "Well, the tests say you have cancer again, but we are gonna fight it." I was beyond upset, beyond!

I said, "I kept telling you this!"

She said the tumor in my chest was very small, and it was missed on the last scan, and I needed to get back to Oakland and do chemo. A few days later, I left Vegas and headed back to Oakland.

CHAPTER 20

— ✂ —

Cancer Strike 3

Keep fighting

I WAS IN shock. Got off the plane and went to my mom's, and the next day was chemo again. Three years in a row, at Christmas time the second time. I was pissed and asked, how could this happen? The blame game.

It didn't matter. I had to kick cancer's ass again, and I had to let my family know again and figure everything out without a job.

This time I just figured if I died of breast cancer, every day I was going to live outside the box. What could I do every day to make me happy?

The doctor said I was stage 4 and I didn't have a lot of time, maybe a year, maybe less than two years. My mind was racing, like, what do you do exactly with limited time? What will really matter?

My second chemo was the day before New Year's 2016. I was on Facebook looking at pictures. Everyone was dressed up and happy, and I was looking at pics with tears coming down my face.

I was like, to heck with all this.

My plan for the new year was to go buy a casket and prepay it, since I had gotten the plot already when Monie was killed. Then I thought, don't go buy a casket. You always wanted a nice car. Go buy a Benz.

The very next day, I went and looked at cars, and two weeks later, I was in a brand-new Mercedes CLA 2016, taking a selfie with a big bright bow, smiling in front of my brand-new car! Yes! No casket, a Benz. I'm crazy, and happy New Year's to me, baby.

Hey, bury me in it later or sell it when I die. All I knew was I was going to start being really carefree, and from that moment I acted like I didn't have cancer. I played a mind game on myself, and it worked. I felt really happy, and I was totally ignoring the fact I was sick and dressed up, and didn't claim death or sickness!

With this kind of chemo, for the second and third time I had cancer, the chemo didn't make me lose all my hair. I kept 90 percent of my hair and got sick half the time, but it was bearable.

I paid all my debts with my severance pay, and I cleaned up my credit. I rolled over my 401(k) into an IRA, and I started investing in stocks, chemo stocks, and did very well for a few months. I was able to help my family and kids, and even though my health was at stake, I was overall happy.

I started decorating my house and looking to buy a house.

I went to Maui and started focusing on having fun and enjoying myself and time with my kids, teaching them things just in case I wouldn't be there. And giving everything to God, which, along the way, I had no choice; I was not in control of this. I never was and never would be.

Along the way, I had to deal with issues with my kids. One of them had a baby, one went to jail, and even though you don't want to worry, you have some stuff to worry about.

Mind you, it's always someone or somebody that has something to say on what I should do or shouldn't do or how I should feel. Come wear my shoes, please and thank you. Would you be able to hang?

After about four months of chemo, I was given two scans and was told I was cancer-free again! And I was able to stop chemo two months early. Yes! I was really happy, and everything seemed like it was going right and like it was going to be OK. God is great!

God gave me really good, excellent intuition; I have always had excellent intuition all my life, so good sometimes I wish I didn't have it. But having it really saved my life.

My mind kept telling me, "You have cancer," even when the doctors kept telling me I didn't. I still didn't believe the doctors, and again I asked a few more times, "Are you sure, no cancer?" I was 95 percent at ease, but a tiny piece of me was not.

PS: Never apologize for trusting your intuition. Our brains can play games, our hearts can be blind, but your gut is always right.

CHAPTER 21

July 19, 2016: Cancer #4

IT WAS MY birthday. "Blow the Whistle" by Too $hort. "I go on and on, can't understand how I last so long, I must have superpowers. Blow the whistle." When I hear that song, I can't help but dance.

Rewind. July 19, 2015, I was cancer-free, on my way to dinner. Now a year had gone by.

The crazy part of this whole crazy cancer stuff is I found the first lump on my birthday four years ago, July 19. My two sisters Faith and Chanel took me out to dinner, and I found a lump before dinner.

Now, four years later, it was my birthday, and for some reason, I was down and sad, so my sister Tiffany took me out to dinner. We went to this nice place, and we got garlic noodles and shrimp, and I ordered two apple martinis. They were so good! For the last four years, I had drunk about three times a year, so I was celebrating, no cancer! I had a great time with my sister!

Later on that night, my chest hurt so bad! The next day, I called the doctor. I asked for another scan, and that day I did a CT scan. A few days later, yep, it's cancer! Are you serious?

I was so hurt, fed up, and just done! All my positive ways went down the drain, and I just got so depressed, and I didn't care anymore. I didn't eat a lot, and I stayed in my room. I lost twenty-seven pounds, and I wanted to give up, and I just cried every day for six weeks. I couldn't talk about it without crying. I couldn't wake up without tears. I turned into a damn crybaby, for real.

That's me in my room right before starting chemo again, thinking of a master plan to all the madness!

My mom and sister helped, and my Moms Lillie (mother-in-law) with the talks.

My daughter asked me a question. "Are you giving up? I never seen you quit before, Mom." That made me think. She said, "Are you gonna quit on us? We need you!"

My sister asked me if I was going to quit. "You have four kids and two grandkids."

Trust me, I do know. I know who loves me, but have you ever been so tired?

I had a moment...and I was back! Never will I quit, but I will stumble. I will fall, but I will get up. I'm counting on my team to lift me up.

I had surgery and removed the grape-sized tumor in my chest and re-covered. I was watching TV a few months ago and went to the bathroom and cut half of my hair off. Over the course of the last few months, I let my hairdresser Andrew cut off the rest of my hair. I had Lynn at the Pamper Bar do my eyebrows for the last time before I lost them. And last month, I let my daughters shave my head again. They did four years ago and could not believe they had to do it again. The bald-headed life for another nine months shouldn't be that bad.

My granddaughter Fallon didn't understand. "How can medicine can make you bald headed?" she said.

"I know, huh?" I had to explain cancer again, and we just took selfies. One minute I was bald headed; the next hour I had a wig on. I guess that's life; you have to make the best of things.

I'm on chemo #5, stage 4, writing a book, the fourth year in a row, the fourth time having cancer.

I'm feeling sick but pushing through. The key to feeling better is drinking lots and lots of fluids: water, smoothies, juices, frozen yogurt, milk shakes. So much going back and forth to the bathroom. It's a lot of work.

Drinking over sixty ounces of fluids or more daily, you don't feel like it, but if you don't, you will be really sick.

I have about another six months left of my treatment plan, four months of chemo and two months of radiation for the first time. Can't wait till it's all over.

The main thing people say to me is, "You beat it three times. You will four times." I know. Look at the bright side, right? Yep, I am.

This is my baby girl Ash, sitting with me while I'm doing chemo. Love her for that. She loves her mom.

I'm praying. I know God has a plan for me and everyone. I never thought I would ever have cancer, let alone four times.

"Cancer" is a scary word, but it also taught me not to be so scary.

I'm tougher than I think. I can be strong. I can let someone help me. It's OK to get help. God's going to take care of me. My kids can take of me.

It's OK. Everything is out of my control and in God's hands.

When they say you will die, that's when you start living, and I just started to live, and I'm not about to die. I will knock this out one more time! Ten more chemos to go!

Cancer, thank you! And good-bye! Forever!

Signed in advance, kicked cancer's ass!

Nese

CHAPTER 22

Resources for New
Cancer Patients

Pray and always ask for help.

—Major Key

To find cancer resources, the first thing you can do is Google breast cancer financial help and resources in your area.

Cleaning for a Reason
http://cleaningforareason.org
Cleaning for a Reason offers cancer patients help with maid services.

The Pink Fund Inc.
http://pinkfund.org

Friends of Faith, the Faith Fancher Breast Cancer Emergency Fund
1-510-601-4040, Oakland / Bay Area
$600 financial support

The Lindy Fund
1-510-420-7900, Oakland / Bay Area
$600 support for low-income women and men for all cancers except breast cancer

American Cancer Society

Susan G. Komen website
http://cancercare.org
Cancer Financial Assistance Coalition
http://cancerfac.org
http://giveitforward.com
Breast Cancer Fund
http://breastcancerfund.org
National Breast Cancer Foundation
http://nationalbreastcancer.org

CHAPTER 23

Pawpaul, Pops, and Grandma Gilda

Grandparents love the kids

I HAD THE very best grandparents, all four of them.

My mom's dad Pawpaul was so cool and nice with me and my sister. He took us everywhere—movies, McDonald's. He let us eat pizza and play the piano and make up songs. He'd pick us up from school and let us watch TV late. He was the best!

He was a family man with older kids, and he was in real estate and was a retired postmaster for the post office.

He loved his kids and grandkids. My heart broke when I found out he had cancer, and he didn't tell anyone until the end.

Watching him die of cancer was completely devastating to me. We found out, and not too much later, he had passed.

I was mad at him, so hurt and mad that he didn't tell me or anybody. I felt time-robbed, and I cried for a long time, and at that time, my sister had just got cancer, so I was really hating cancer and not understanding, why my family? I wish you could have stayed a little while longer. RIP.

Pops was my dad's father, a real estate investor and businessman. He owned a home in the Hayward Hills, in the Kelly Hill neighborhood. He was so sweet and kind to me and all the grandkids.

Pops went to Italy for the war and married and brought back my grandma Gilda.

Pops and I had a very special relationship with ice cream. We loved it, so much so he had a big freezer in the garage with at least twenty gallons of different kinds, and we would try them out.

He was the life of the party. He was really a true-life Sammy Davis Jr. He would drink and smoke a lot, and when my parents told me he had cancer, it broke my heart!

Remembering back, we always had Sunday dinner and pizza parties, music, and dancing. We would step it out. Happy days.

The crazy part was watching him suffer; that hurt. The day he passed, I was in his room, and he whispered in my ear, "Make me some ice cream." I smiled and laughed and said OK. When I came back with the ice cream, he had passed away. Tears. I hate cancer!

Till this day I love ice cream mainly because of Pops. Love you, Pops. Both my grandfathers gone to cancer, wow.

My grandma Gilda was a very beautiful Italian woman and a very hardworking businesswoman who worked very hard, and she would make her grandkids help her. She was not playing about working.

If Grandma was mad, she would curse you out in Italian. We wouldn't know what she was saying, had no clue. But we knew to run. She would slap the mess out you. She would crack up laughing.

She was a great cook and she loved her beers, *Jeopardy*, *Wheel of Fortune*, and *The Golden Girls*. Please don't mess with her while those shows were on.

Grandma Gilda gave out lots of kisses and hugs. She and Pops liked to dress up and go out! A night on the town!

After Pops passed, the family kept her company, and she had a few best friends that visited with her.

Years later, when Grandma got cancer, I stayed with her and helped her. She had a brain tumor, and after surgery she wasn't the same. She later went into hospice, and seeing what cancer did again was heartbreaking, to say the least. I would visit a lot, but sometimes, I couldn't bear to see her suffer. She also passed away from cancer.

Grandma taught me so much. The main thing is don't be lazy, work hard, and love family. RIP, Grandma.

Seeing all three of my grandparents die from three different kinds of cancer was terrible. The crazy thing is they say cancer does not run in my family. Interesting.

Love them while they are still here. I wish I had a grandparent. Miss and love you all.

Rest in peace.

CHAPTER 24

— ✿ —

Maui, Maui, Hawaii, Hawaii: Bye, Kids

I'M OUT! AUDI 5000, G.

I was at the Oakland, California, airport. It was my very first real trip without kids, just me, Ny-Ny, my cuz Berta, and my friends Nichelle and Nakia. We were meeting up in Hawaii, yes! I was super excited!

I'm scared of planes, but I got my butt on the plane. It wasn't so bad. When I landed, Ny-Ny and Nichelle picked me up from the airport. So beautiful. It was raining but still very beautiful.

This was my second time to Hawaii. My first time my sister was granted a wish from the Make-a-Wish Foundation, and they granted us a trip to Hawaii, all expenses paid, but that was thirty years ago, so yeah, I was excited!

We went grocery shopping and stayed in a condo near everything. We ate a lot of food and had drinks and went shopping. We hit up a wine tasting and got some good wine.

We took pictures and went to a luau. It was very nice, but we left early. It started to rain really hard.

Kia, Ny-Ny, and me, Maui chillin'

The boardwalk in Maui is so relaxing. I loved to watch the water and play in the sand. I got in the water with the girls and turned around, and a giant sea turtle was behind me. Yeah, I had to get out. I don't swim well. I had a great time. We tried a lot of food places and very nice restaurants and had a blast on Mother's Day!

Nichelle, Kia, and me taking selfies

We stayed a week and did a lot of sight-seeing and more shopping at the outlets and went to mall. You know I love to shop, and I did a lot more sleeping in and relaxing. You have to recover from eating and shopping.

We got some henna tattoos. Some days the weather was really warm, and we got shaved ice, hecka good. Got a massage. Nothing like just chilling!

We ended the trip by going to a fancy restaurant for Ny-Ny's birthday, and it was really nice, and the food was great!

Me and my cuzn Berta, chillin'

I had a very nice time with the ladies, and it made me think, why haven't I been jumping on planes? Time to jet set and see the world (you too, reader). It feels good to get away!

Boarding the plane, looking out the window, bye-bye, Maui. See you next year!

CHAPTER 25

—— ✂ ——

God and Prayers

Don't forget to pray

I LOVE GOD. God has been a blessing in my life. Through all the turns and troubles and ups and downs, God has always pulled me through! Talking to God and praying, I really learned to build a closer relationship with him, and as I got older, I truly believe in the power of prayer.

Ask God, believe and trust, really trust, and lean on him in hard times. Don't depend on yourself to get yourself through. You have to give it to God.

Jehovah has blessed me and my children and always answered right on time. The only way I have made it this far is through Jehovah and his love!

Some say that God puts only so much on those that can bear it, and I must be a very strong women. But I'm not as strong as people think, because I know God is carrying my weight.

Maybe my story is to be told for someone to pull through something—maybe, maybe not. But all I can say is if you pray and talk to God, he will listen.

Sometimes we don't get everything we ask for. Sometimes God gives us the superstrength to push through battles. I never in a million years would have thought I would have cancer, let alone four different times, but that's my story, and I'm pushing through.

I'm on chemo #3 now, and I've decided I'm going to get this book done with God's help and no excuses, no complaints.

I'm writing and pushing through the pain, the hard times, but finding peace, joy, and light at the end of the dark tunnel as well.

I know God has a purpose for all of us and me, and I'm walking in it as we speak. While walking our journeys in life, let's not forgot somebody somewhere has it way worse than we do, and we could be not breathing. Life is a blessing, so if you're stressing, like I know how to stress—trust me: been there, done that—just remember God hears prayers.

When I was young, I prayed to God. I had gotten into the habit of repeating prayers as if he didn't already know I had said them, over and over. Sometimes God sent someone to help me, but when I really poured my heart out and talked to God, those prayers were answered.

It's so important to teach your children how to pray. That helps them learn how to count on God to help them with problems that they may not want to tell us parents.

Praying as a single woman and a single mother has helped ease a lot of burdens that I would try to do alone. So many thousands and thousands of prayers, I would have to say, "Jehovah, it's me again, I know, I know...it's Trinese again."

Always keep God in your heart through the good and great times and trials and tribulations. Stay strong!

Love,

Nese

CHAPTER 26

— ⚘ —

Happiness

If there were a store that sold happiness, how much would you buy?

My grandson Carter and me, my happiness

Happiness, happy feelin's! Happy feelin's in the air!

—MAZE

I LOVE MUSIC! It makes me happy; I love to cook and clean to music.

When you get dressed for work and put on some music, it sets the day for you to have a good day and good mood.

When I started writing this book, I noticed there were a lot of painful and unhappy moments in my life, and I told my daughter, "I don't have a lot of happiness in my life."

She said, "Yeah, you been through a lot, Mom."

It made me think, what exactly makes me happy? The little things. Flowers and candles, my grandkids, my granddaughter Fallon—she's a little ole lady who has so much joy—and my grandson Carter, who is a cute, sweet baby. Family makes me happy.

Having my four kids and seeing them grow up and graduate school, I'm loving that. It makes me feel proud to see my babies, now all eighteen years old and older, being adults and finding out how to be happy and experiencing life and how they can find happiness on their own.

It's true: everyone is in charge of his or her own happiness. I make a point to do things by myself that make me happy, and it feels good.

Life is short! Live and be happy! Do you and do you happy! There are too many miserable people. I wasn't happy with my life, my money, my credit, my weight, my job, my relationship, and sometimes my kids' ways and choices. But with all that being said, if you don't make changes to be happy, you stay in the same (unhappy) life. And next thing you know, it's been five years, ten years. When will you make a change to be happy? Maybe next year, maybe for the new year.

Sometimes we settle in life and never get the real happiness we deserve, because we don't have faith and haven't been happy in so long that we become accustomed to the way life is.

Hey, I dare you to be happy on purpose!

I dare you to take that jump to success!

Write down three goals, and check them off as you go! Start to exercise, and keep going and keep doing. It will make you happy to see changes.

Change happens when we change. I'm changing for the better, no matter what obstacles come my way.

I never want to take my happiness for granted. Get up, blast the music, and dance. Even when you don't feel like it, dance anyway. There's nothing like turning on your favorite song.

How happy are you now? Think about it and take action, boss! Time waits for no one, no one! Be happy, and claim everything you deserve!

Singing "Because I'm Happy," by Pharrell.

CHAPTER 27

Today

Do it today...tomorrow isn't promised

LIFE IS CRAZY.

Life is full of changes. Life is unexpected. Life is good. It's do or die, sink or swim, positive or negative, highs and lows, ups and down. Life can beat you up, or life can be great. One thing's for sure: we all have different fates.

We all have a book of life, with different chapters. Some chapters are full and big, and some chapters are small but very eventful.

Whatever book God gave you, write the best days of your life, and appreciate it. I mean really appreciate this gift called life.

Be careful how you think of yourself. So it shall be, sometimes.

Today if you're sad and down, get your hair done, get a haircut, put on some perfume or cologne. If you don't like what you have become, make the changes to become the very best you!

If you don't like how you look, start making changes. Changes don't start until you change the way you feel and see yourself, and once you see changes, things start changing!

Today, be your best. Even when you're not at your best, the best investment you can make is in yourself.

Today, think of the positive. Pray for the positive life. Stay positive and around positive people, and the positive is on its way. Positive energy is flowing our way!

Today, work on your dream. How is your dream going to come true if you don't work on it? Make it happen, Captain!

Today, take care of your health.

Today, be real to yourself. Nothing like smiling with a lump in your throat. When you say to yourself, "I'm fine, I'm OK," and you're not, you're not really being real to your own self, let alone keeping it real with others. Once you keep it real, the help is on its way. Sometimes even I had to hang up my own cape and keep it real, needed someone to take care of me for a change.

Today, get up and get active! Get happy! Make yourself happy! What are we waiting for? Dress yourself up. Hey, go buy your own flowers! Put on some MAC lipstick. Buy some candles; ice cream works too. Put on some music, and dance your butt off while cooking. Read a book. Shopping always brings a smile to my face. Walk the lake! Go out to dinner with friends.

Now we are going to get up and get happy, baby! Enjoy life today.

Today! I didn't take full advantage of today until I was told I might not be around after five years. Then I was trying to cram so much in a day. What I did learn was I am not in control; God is.

Every day is a blessing. Make God proud today! And don't forget to pray today.

PS: This chapter is based on iPhone notes I wrote the first time I was doing chemo to remind myself not to give up.

So what are you going to do with your today that you didn't do yesterday? Because today is today, and tomorrow isn't promised.

CHAPTER 28

My Heartbeats

A mother's love

ALWAYS WANTED TO be a mom. Never thought I would be a single mom, but after 2005, I was. I always thought I would be married forever with my four kids. Never knew all this was going to happen.

But it did. When I became a mom at eighteen, I made a promise to myself that I would sacrifice what I wanted in life to take care of my son, and I did. I finished school, and for almost four years, it was just Lil Monie and me, living at my parents' house. His dad and I both took care of him. His dad lived at Grandma Margie's, and we would alternate weeks, so it wasn't so bad.

And I had help from my sister, Grandma Lillie, my mom Nana, Auntie Jackie, my cousin Michelle, my little sisters Faith and Chanel, and Auntie Phaedra, so I had a hand with my firstborn. He was a little independent man who was a character, with a big tummy.

As a mom, you want to protect your kids always, and I can't lie: I have worried and stressed over my kids many, many nights. I've said many prayers asking for God to help me be a good mother and guide me through.

At eighteen, having a baby matured me more, and I went to school and handled my business. All the help from the family helped a lot, and every weekend it seemed like everyone wanted Lil Monie to spend the night, so I was pretty free to work. For almost four years, it was just Lil Jamonie, Big Jamonie, and me, and motherhood wasn't so bad.

We had a lot of fun together and lots of Chuck E. Cheese parties, and you could say my firstborn was a daddy's boy but also a momma's boy too.

Lil Monie did very well in school and sports, and it wasn't until his dad's untimely death that he went into another direction, and unfortunately I couldn't reach him and his very hurt heart. Losing his dad at fourteen years of age and being shot with his dad really changed him, and he didn't really care anymore.

He loved to rap, and he made music. Before his father was killed, I had him go downstairs, and I told him, "Learn all you can from those producers down there." I said that every day, and it paid off.

It had been a few months since his dad had died, and I was broke, waiting on my disability check, and he said, "Mom, I'll be right back in a few hours." He came back, and he had sold some of his music, his beats, and made $1,200. I was very impressed.

So Lil Monie said, "Mom, here, I want you to have this money."

I couldn't take it but said, "Hey, why don't you do this? Go into Safeway, take your brother and sisters, get two baskets, and shop for some food."

I parked outside and watched them shop, and they were having fun getting all these snacks. But when they got to the car, they said, "Hey, Mom, we got you some stuff you would like." I thought that was very thoughtful, and it made me cry that they were even thinking of me.

Being a single mom was made easier with certain people that helped, and I really appreciated that, especially Unc Leon and Auntie Phaedra, Grandpa Edward and Grandma Lillie, and my mom, sister, brother and my dad,& Joffre.

Unfortunately, I also had unwanted help from a few people that would steer my sons in the wrong direction and couldn't have cared less about it. They would smile in my face, but behind my back they meant a lot of harm to my kids. They didn't care if they went to school or if they were in the right environment. They wanted to give them drugs and have them drugged out and then ask, "What's wrong with them? Why are they failing in life? If they daddy was here, that wouldn't be happening!" Sure wouldn't.

I'm crazy about my kids and love them to pieces, so yes, I'm the mom that pops up at the school all the time and looks at you in the little window. I'm the mom that will drag you into the car from somewhere you're not supposed to be. I will tell you right from wrong a thousand times and, if you need to hear it, a thousand times more. I won't give up on you.

I have a rule with myself as far as my kids are concerned: I never make promises I don't keep, period. So when someone makes promises to my kids and breaks them, now that is where I don't play around with, and yes, that has been the case.

What people fail to realize is once you make promises and don't follow through, it lets the child down. And this was one problem as a single mom I hated to see. It was always a nice gesture, but people sometimes write checks they can't cash, and this always seemed to happen with my sons and people who wanted to play father figures. Granted, I loved that a few tried to step up to the plate, but I didn't like to see my son disappointed, especially when it came to him reaching his music dreams.

My kids' dad thought if anything ever happened to him, at least fifty people would have my back. Then he would name his top ten. Sad to say, that wasn't the case; people get busy with life and have their own kids and bills and lives. Some people he mentioned, sad to say, I haven't seen since he died, and that was eleven years ago.

Not to bash anyone, but real talk, keeping it one thousand, I learned who some people really were. Listen, I had someone trying to talk to me, my husband's friend. Now my apartment had just been broken into, and I moved to a nicer place by the lake. On that day I was thinking, man, I just blew through some money. I had to pay rent at my old place and then pay first and last plus deposit at the new spot, so it was about $5,500. Then I had to pay bills, and I had to buy new furniture. So I was getting down to a few thousand in my bank account.

I went to walk around the lake to not even think about it, and I saw a childhood friend. He was my friend and Monie's friend, so I thought he was cool; plus he was a married millionaire.

I told him my house had been burglarized, and he said, "Hey, I will pay all your bills, rent, and add ten thousand a month, but you can't see anyone. You only have to see me three or four times a month."

I said, "Wow, so when did I become a ho to you? Which day?"

"Stay broke then."

"I have a great job! Thank you!"

"Well, stay struggling then!"

I was in shock, and we ended our conversation, but before I left, I told him, "Wow, he thought you were his friend for sure." Shaking my head.

The real crazy part was a few hours later, another friend of Monie's called me and offered me $10,000 a month. I sat back laughing so hard with the phone on mute. No, thank you! $25,000 a month to deal with two men for a week out of the month? Yeah, I will stay at my desk job and keep my soul, thank you!

Now I told that story because in the real world, somebody would have taken that money, for real. But I wasn't raised like that. And that friend was just a little bit of some of the BS that I had to deal with as a single mother.

Being a single mother meant working and hustling, clothes, earrings, purses, peach cobbler, lots and lots of peach cobbler, going to the casino, but taking money from men was not my MO, and I didn't even want my kids asking my boyfriend at the time for any money, didn't want anyone to ever throw that in my face.

But I have to admit my boyfriend Joffr'e really helped on his own when I didn't ask him to. He had my back for many years. If I didn't have something and he knew I wasn't going to ask, he would handle it. Especially for my kids' birthdays, he always went way out and did stuff over the top.

I really appreciated that we had each other's back and he was someone that they could talk to and that would be a friend to them as well. He never tried to replace their dad. He did step up to the plate as a father figure, and they always talk about him, even though we parted ways.

My heartbeats—that picture sums it up. My four kids, my nieces KK and Angel and nephew Doodah, and my grandkids.

My next two kids I will talk about are Ashley and Paris.

Ashley was born with bright-red hair and was my little strawberry shortcake. She helped me so much. She was the little lady of the house. While I worked, she helped with her brother and sister, picking them up after school.

She was a daddy's girl for sure! Ashley really never gave me too much headache. I would just buy her some Vans or Jordans for the help, and she was cool.

Ashley is a very loving sister, and she was heartbroken by her dad's death. I was very proud of Ashley when she graduated high school, and I'm sure she will be successful with whatever business she decides to open. I know that if anything should ever happen to me with this cancer, Ashley will be responsible enough to make it and be there for her siblings.

That's Paris, my P, my red man. Paris was ten pounds when he was born. Need I say more? He had the closest relationship with his dad, and he took his death the hardest.

Being a single mom brings challenges, but Paris was a handful, and it was hard raising him. He was angry at the whole world for his dad's death, and that also included me. Paris is a very smart, sweet teddy bear who has a hurt soul. If I could bring back his dad, I would bring him back for Lil P.

Paris taught me to never give up. He taught me to fight. I wasn't going to lose him to the streets. He loved football and music. But once his dad was gone, he didn't play sports anymore. As years went by, the one thing I wished I could give Paris was happiness. He was so unhappy without his dad. I love his smile.

When we argue in a joking kind of way, he says, "Tell ya about them blondes," and I say, "Tell ya about them reds." We have a love/hate relationship, but we both are each other's number one fan.

In the past his decisions about his friends and whom he has had in his life have been big mistakes that he is learning from right now. I know that God has a plan for Paris, and I can't wait to see what that is.

My baby Aaliyah, a.k.a. Nini—my last baby is now eighteen years old and graduated, and she has a little son named Carter. A few people wanted me to give up on her since she became a teen mom, but I didn't! Seeing her grow up to be a great mom that handles her business reminds me of me, and we had to prove some people wrong! Hi, haters! When you are young, you make mistakes, but it's what you do after the mistakes that counts. At least that's how I see it.

Out of all my kids, I know if I get old, Nini will take care of me. She has been a very, very big help over the last four years of my cancer treatment, and I really appreciate that, and I'm really proud of her!

Nini, don't let anything stand in your way, single mom or not, baby!

Before I had kids, my little brother John was my first real-life doll. He was my little baby, and he is a big part of my heartbeat, my twin.

My nieces and nephew are Auntie's little babies, eating ice cream! Love them, my niece KK and my cupcake Lana.

Having children, I would always look for mentors to help them along the way: Grandpa John, Grandpa Edward, and Grandpa Greg.

My sisters-in-law have always been helpful: Faith and Chanel and Antionette. Without them it would have been a harder journey.

My kids' angel has been their cousin Jimmy. He always looked out for them, and we really appreciate him helping us through some very hard times.

One of my husband's friends and my friend as well from junior high, Damon Garder, always made it a point to pay for my sons' haircuts for many years, even when he didn't have to, or look after them at games. That was really appreciated.

I put mentors in place for my daughter Ashley, my friends Shane Wayne and Taylor. Shane taught her a lot about having a business, and Taylor also showed her a lot of skills working in their bakery.

Now that all my kids are grown, I love not having to deal with school-age kids. I'm learning to let them be grown and fly the nest. I miss my little babies. I wish I could rewind and start over. I know that the main reason I'm kicking cancer's butt is for them, my heartbeats.

Family makes single motherhood worth it!

Shout out to Grandma Margie, RIP. She helped so much in helping raise my kids as they grew up. She loved her great-grandkids to pieces. We love and miss you!

The single mom's job is never done. But the job is well worth it! We love hard, we work hard, and everything is for our kids, our heartbeats. A mother's love. XOXOXO

CHAPTER 29

A Piece of Nese

A.k.a. Trinese—7/19

PLAYING "CLOSER" BY Goapele, closer to my dreams. I'm getting higher and higher. Love that song.

Who is Nese? Trinese, raised in Oakland, California.

East Oakland

She loves. She's loveable. She's loyal and faithful. She is light and bright. She shines. She's a star. She's tough as a tiger. She is soft and kind. She endures and maintains. She's social but a loner. She is smart and has passion. She is thankful and grateful.

She has been built and rebuilt. Her heart is broken but mended. She forgives but remembers.

She is giving and freehearted. She makes mistakes and owns them. She is a sister, mother, daughter, friend, and niece.

She's perfect and so imperfect but perfectly made by God. She's so quiet and shy but can be loud and funny. She is a fighter, a survivor. She is a raider, a warrior.

If you were to make a poem about yourself, what would it say?

Try it!

Welcome to my world!

Thanks for reading about pieces of my life, not in order, from the brain of a slightly touched dyslexic lady.

As a child, I collected puzzles, and I had hundreds of them, from a ten-piece to a fifty-thousand-piece puzzle. If I lose a piece, I won't put that puzzle up until I find it.

When you see things a little backward, you unfortunately do things backward, and you constantly check your work to make sure you didn't spell something backward, especially numbers and dates. The good thing is it makes you want to be perfect, and you recheck everything.

Life is one big puzzle, and my life has been affected by so many different things: God, prayers, gun violence, cancer, rape, depression, love, relationships, kids and grandkids, money, work, bills, survival—all pieces to my life.

Trinese is a girl raised in Oakland by two loving parents and a family, who ended up having four kids and went through gun violence and cancer and is still trying to survive.

Jamonie, a.k.a. Monie, was raised by a loving family, and he loved his family and kids and made decisions that affected his life.

We were just a young couple that got married, and the fairy-tale ending wasn't our story, but I know that Jamonie made a lot of choices for his kids, and he really loved us.

I have been writing my book over the last eight years, and sometimes my life story was too much for me, let alone putting it out there for the whole world to see, so I procrastinated. Procrastination is something I am working on, and I promised myself I won't let that distract me from any dreams I have.

I hope you enjoyed my story.

Don't wait on life. Start living life now.

Peace,

Nese

XOXOXO

Special Shout-Outs and Thank-Yous

TO MY MOM, Toya Alexander, and Aunt Tammy, my sister Tiffany and Curt, Moms Lillie, Aunt Phaedra, Dominque Suber, Grandma Margie, Yoshii, Tosha, Erica, Valencia, Dari, Olfe, Keisha, Momma Keisha, Brenda, Tamika and Antionette, the Tullis family

Ny-Ny-Naima, Berta Jean, Monique Rhodes, Auntie Eldora and Auntie Jackie, Michelle and May Young, my dad, Unc Charlie, Lil Charlie, my brother John, Grandpa Edward and Greg Robinson, Phaedra and Leon Watson, Keyjonte, Antionette Robinson, Uncle Raymond, Eric and Bobby, Mr. King CC, Shane and Taylor

Thanks to

The Robinson family, the Howell family, the Alexander family, the Watson family, the Grant family, the Williamsons, the Rollins family, the Holmes, the Emerys, and the Blackwells

The Oakland Dynamites

The Lawsons, the Gardner family

The Tims family

The Ferrell family, the Turner and Thorton family, Mr. Malone, Mr. Squarebear, Kwame and Anthony, the Pearson family, Stanley Cox aka Mistah Fab

Highland and Kaiser emergency staff

Thanks to the many doctors and nurses

My friend and attorney, Kurt Robinson

Elo Ray, Lavita, my AT&T family, Lakeshore and Eastshore, the Gizers, Janet, Sharon Tessa, Kalem, Keilon, Joffr'e, Aisha, Eureka, T. Guy, Toni, Angie B., Nakia, Leon, Kristen, Kim, Deja, Nikole, Toni Lynn, Dalinda, Shona, Carisa, Danielle and Denisha, Michelle Pierre, Janet Johnson, Sharon Smith, Dezi, Gail, Fam Bam, my cousin Tantosha, Auntie Cynthia, and the Ellis family

Kenya and Brandi, XOXOXO

Kimberley and Ashonti, Keta Foster

The Brown and Mason family

My kids, Ashley, Jamonie, Paris, and Aaliyah

My sisters-in-law, Faith and Chanel, XOXO

My grandbabies, Carter and Fallon, Mika

Auntie's babies, Cupcake, Doodah, and KK, and Angel, Lil Paris, and Raul

Love you guys and so many other family and friends. Much XOXOXO to Oakland and the Bay Area.

Rest in peace, Jamonie. We miss you.

Special thanks to my mom and aunt. Love you!
Wishing you love, joy, and happiness, health, and wealth, Love,
Nese
PS. Never lose your sense of humor.
A Piece of Nese: Made in Oakland

About the Author

TRINESE ROBINSON'S DEBUT book, *A Piece of Nese...Made in Oakland*, recounts her life as a citizen of troubled Oakland, California, through its darkest hours. Gun violence and cancer takes a toll on her life.

Robinson has four children and two grandchildren. She hopes to inspire and motivate others by sharing her personal and spiritual journey.

53861402R00101

Made in the USA
San Bernardino, CA
30 September 2017